celtic
knotwork
handbook

CELTIC KNOTWORK HANDBOOK

Sheila Sturrock

GUILD OF MASTER CRAFTSMAN PUBLICATIONS LTD

This edition published 1999 by
Guild of Master Craftsman Publications Ltd,
166 High St, Lewes,
East Sussex BN7 1XU

Copyright © Guild of Master Craftsman Publications Ltd
Text copyright © Sheila Sturrock 1999

Reprinted 2000 (twice)

ISBN 1 86108 115 4

British Library Cataloguing in Publication Data.
A catalogue record of this book is available from the British Library

The publishers would like to thank: the Manchester Metropolitan
University for their kind permission to reproduce the Eternal
Knot and Celtic Cross designs on pages 3 and 8, both from the
Laura Seddon Collection.

Illustrations by Guild of Master Craftsman
Publications Design Studio 1997

Cover and interior designed by Wheelhouse Design
Typefaces: Cantoria, Sabon and Omnia

Colour origination by Viscan Graphics (Singapore)
Printed in Hong Kong by H&Y Printing Ltd

Acknowledgements

It would be impossible to produce a book of this type without the assistance of people willing to test the designs. A very special thankyou must go to Carole Harrison, Read Primary School, who kindly 'lent' me her class to teach, and to Jack Dowling, Smallbridge Primary School, Rochdale, who passed on his enthusiasm to his own class with outstanding results. Thankyou to Val Fynan and the East Lancashire Calligraphy Group for their encouragement and support.

CONTENTS

INTRODUCTION

T his book has been written for all those people who have tried plotting Celtic knotwork but have, as yet, failed, and for all craft workers who wish to use Celtic knotwork in their designs. There are books of ready-made designs which are excellent, but these do not teach the essential element of construction which enables students to combine designs and adapt them to their own requirements, as did the ancient scribes.

I developed my method of construction out of frustration, and quite by chance. Having failed to follow other methods I drew hearts, which are a common design feature, over a sheet of paper and joined them by extending diagonal lines from their centres. This produced a knotwork design, and I found that by varying the placement of hearts and joining lines, different designs were produced. I then moved on to starting with larger hearts, which gave me the space for more interweaving, then modified the hearts by extending the base and the top. Each change in the basic heart led to different designs and different effects.

By breaking knotwork down into a series of curves and lines, plotting all the curves on squared graph paper, and then joining them together with lines, the construction became simple, with no need for complicated measurements and counting. Curves and lines make up the two basic units of all designs plotted using this technique – hearts and loops – so anyone who can draw a simple heart and interweave correctly will have no difficulty in executing what appear to be very complicated patterns.

I have divided the book into chapters according to the basic construction unit of the designs, for example, all the patterns in Chapter 3 are constructed by first plotting a series of small hearts. Examples in each chapter demonstrate the different effects that can be produced through various ways of plotting curves and lines.

All the patterns illustrated are based on angles of 45°, 90°, and 180°, where traditional designs are much more flexible. The ancient scribes simply extended lines or pointed loops to fill irregular shapes. Once the basic principle in each chapter has been understood, you can experiment with plotting shapes in different positions, and move away from rigid plottings, adapting patterns to suit any size or shape required. Similarly, once the idea of zoomorphics (animal forms) becomes familiar, any animal, plant or man can be fashioned out of a convenient curve.

The designs illustrated are plotted on a grid of dots rather than on a graph to prevent possible confusion from too many lines. In each chapter designs are presented according to the number of squares required for a test design (a single draft of the complete design), commencing with the least number of squares across and down and gradually increasing in width and depth. This enables the reader to mark out an accurate grid for the test piece, and to select a design to fit the space available for decoration. The ordering is *not* according to difficulty. A design which uses a small number of squares is not necessarily less complex than a design which uses a large number. A square can be any size, so a design which requires eight squares across and five down is equally suited to a space of 8 x 5in (marked in 1in squares) or 40 x 25mm (marked in 5mm squares).

What is important is that the space can be divided into the number of squares required to fit the particular design. Plotting exact graphs becomes less important as confidence is gained, and designs can be drawn over a few lightly pencilled dots.

Celtic cross decorated with a celtic knotwork design.

PART ONE

Tools & Techniques

Chapter 1

ḣistory

The Celts

During the seventh century BC, Celts from the Continent began to arrive and settle in Britain. Celtic kings were often patrons of the arts, and the Celts are still known for their art, fine ornaments and jewellery. Their knotwork and interlacing patterns in particular are instantly recognized.

Knotwork was both a decorative and a religious art, borne from the oral traditions of the Celtic people and the beliefs they learned from the Druids. Celtic art had three main functions:

- depiction of stories;
- decoration; and
- religious symbolism.

According to Celtic beliefs, there are seven created life forms – plant, insect, fish, reptile, bird, mammal and man.

These are all represented in Celtic art, but in a stylized and highly imaginative form, as to copy the art of the creator was forbidden. Human figures (anthropomorphics) depict men with interlaced limbs and extended beards, and animal forms (zoomorphics) are shown with extended and interweaving ears, tails and tongues.

Plaitwork and knotwork designs

Knotwork is developed from plaitwork. Plaitwork patterns consist of straight, diagonal lines joined together with curves, as in the example shown in Fig 1.1. They were used extensively in Roman, Greek and Egyptian art. (There are many patterns in Chapter 12,

Straight Lines, which show how plait-work can be developed into knotwork.)

In the sixth century AD, plaitwork was used extensively in Italian churches to decorate altar screens and covers for various church vessels. The plaitwork

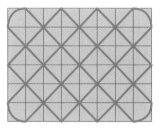

FIG 1.1 Roman plaitwork.

decorations of this time show a development from the early designs that opened up greater possibilities for the creation of more intricate patterns. Instead of using continuous diagonal lines, they used broken lines, which enabled interweaving.

The Celts also used broken lines in their own distinctive, interwoven knotwork (see Fig 1.2). Because they used their knotwork to decorate irregular

spaces on stone crosses, manuscripts, jewellery and wood, they also added angular lines and pointed loops to fill in corners, and used a variety of motifs to close off knotwork ribbons. In this way, even the simplest ribbon could be woven into intricate patterns producing secondary ribbons, which were sometimes highlighted by using a different colour for each lacing.

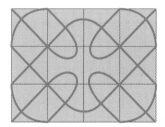

FIG 1.2 Celtic knotwork showing the break in lines in the centre.

Spirals and key patterns are also characteristic of Celtic knotwork design (see Figs 1.3 and 1.4). Spirals were the earliest motifs used in Celtic Christian art. They are patterns composed of

FIG 1.3 Spiral patterns are common in knotwork designs.

Materials

The designs were created using simple materials. Lines were drawn with the quill of a goose or crow feather, both of which could be fashioned to give a square end with a very fine point, and the designs were then scored using a stylus made from wood, iron or bone. (It is possible that silver points were also

circles (the circle being the symbol of perfection) which are joined together with shallow, elongated S- or C-shaped curves. Key patterns resemble the notches of a key, the most recognizable of these being the Greek key pattern which appears to be a 'square' spiral, but

FIG 1.4 A typical key pattern.

is, in fact, a series of short horizontal and vertical lines. Celtic key patterns differ from this in that they also incorporate diagonal lines in the designs. All key patterns are made up of straight lines.

FIG 1.5 Example of an eternal knot design. These were very popular at the start of the nineteenth century.

used.) Vellum was used for manuscripts. The difficulties of writing on a hairy surface such as this were overcome by the fineness and shape of the quill point. Writing on a hairy surface is rather like drawing with pen on a pile carpet. The square end of the quill allowed it to travel down through the vellum pile which enabled the scribe to draw on the actual skin rather than on the fine fibres.

With the design plotted, further details were superimposed in light coloured ink. Colour was applied to the edges with a quill, and large areas were coloured using a brush. Designs were sometimes highlighted by leaving small areas of the work unpainted.

Colours

Celtic artists had an astonishing knowledge of the chemical properties of pigments and their manuscripts were alive with vibrant colour. Many pigments were obtained from local sources: red from red lead; yellow (orpiment) from soil found in parts of Ireland; emerald green from copper; violet blue from the woad plant (also known as 'dyer's weed'); whites from white lead and chalk; and verdigris, a greenish-blue from a patina formed on copper, brass or bronze. Other pigments were imported: mauves, maroons and purples are thought to have been obtained from the Mediterranean plant *Crozophora tinctoria*; kermes (crimson) was produced from the pregnant bodies of insects *(Kermococcus vermilio)* that lived in the evergreen trees of the Mediterranean; and ultramarine, a rare and valuable pigment of brilliant blue, thought to have been obtained by crushing lapis lazuli, which was imported from the foothills of the Himalayas in north-east Afghanistan. Indigo, an oriental plant, was the source of a deeper blue.

Chapter 2

ϻaterials & Techniques

MATERIALS

The materials required for Celtic knotwork are few and inexpensive.

Plotting

Graph paper is essential. I recommend 5mm squares as a convenient size for trying out most patterns and 1cm squares for complicated designs where a number of lines interweave, as a larger drawing makes it much easier to see each crossing point. Once the interweaving has been understood the actual work can be done on any size square.

Grids can easily be transferred from graph paper to plain paper by securing a plain sheet over the graph paper with masking tape, and using the squares to draw a grid on the plain sheet (see Fig 2.1).

A 2B pencil is best for plotting the designs as the lines produced are clear and the soft lead can be rubbed out easily once the design has been inked in. An

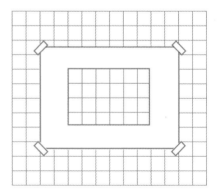

Fig 2.1 Attach plain paper to a background piece of squared paper with masking tape, and use the squares to draw a grid in the required position.

0.5mm automatic pencil is invaluable for this work. An automatic pencil allows a continuous supply of lead which does not vary in thickness and does not require constant sharpening as does a normal pencil. The 0.5mm lead combines strength with accuracy – the finer 0.3mm breaks too easily while the 0.7mm does not give the fineness and accuracy required.

Colouring

Water-soluble pencils have a waxy texture and give a good depth of colour which is easily controlled. After the design has been coloured in, water can be painted over the pencil marks to give the effect of a water-colour design – subtle shading can be introduced in this way. Felt-tip pens can be used to give an interesting shaded effect to ribbonwork, especially in large designs where the colour 'overlaps'.

Outlining

To outline the designs, use a black fibre-tip pen. These come in a variety of widths and are available from stationers and art shops. As a general guide, choose a fine tip for small designs and a thicker tip for larger ones, although the choice will depend upon the effect you require: if only a small space is required for filling in with colour, outlining a small design with a thick tip would be an appropriate choice. Fibre-tip pens are also useful for filling in backgrounds and to produce various effects such as stoning and graining.

BASIC PLOTTING TECHNIQUES

Curves and lines

All knotwork can be broken down into a series of curves and lines which make up the two basic units of all patterns plotted using this technique – hearts and loops. The curves are based on parts of a circle (i.e. quarter, half, three-quarter or full) and may be drawn either outside or inside the grid squares. Straight lines are drawn at angles of 45°, 90° or 180° to the vertical. (See Figs 2.2–2.4.)

Fig 2.2 Curves outside a square.

Fig 2.3 Curves inside a square.

Fig 2.4 Lines at 45°, 90° and 180° to the vertical.

Plotting the design

While there are various ways of plotting the curves to produce different effects, a general process can be applied to the plotting of all knotwork patterns. Following just the first two steps listed will produce the basic line work, and following all six will give a knotwork design of ribbons.

1 Plot all the curves.

2 Add the straight lines.

3 Apply ribbonwork by chosen method.

4 Identify crossing points for interweaving.

5 Ink in outlines.

6 Erase construction lines.

Draw the basic construction curves and lines on graph paper. This drawing will show the crossing points and also the smallest space in the design, so that the interweaving and appropriate width for the ribbon can be determined. Once this has been done, the lines can be converted to ribbonwork.

Figure 2.30 shows four individual ribbons of equal width, which interweave. The maximum thickness of these ribbons is determined by the size of the centre square (the smallest space): half the width of each ribbon = half the width of the centre square.

Interweaving

Interweaving occurs when two lines cross each other: one must pass over or under the other. This is represented in knotwork by breaking the line which passes underneath. (See Figs 2.5 and 2.6.) Adding lines to the design increases the interweaving (see Figs 2.7 and 2.8), and when each line is joined

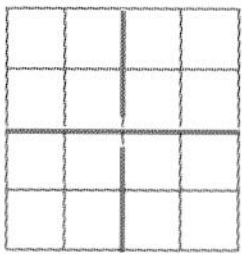

FIG 2.6 The broken line indicates that the vertical line passes underneath the horizontal line.

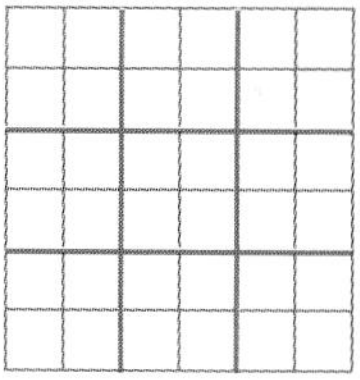

FIG 2.7 Four crossing lines.

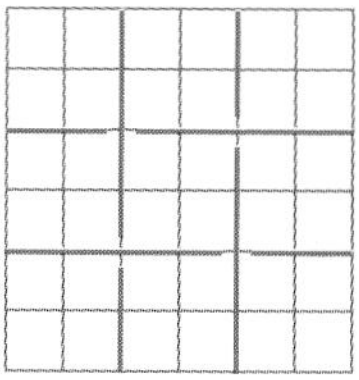

FIG 2.8 Broken lines indicate which lines pass underneath.

FIG 2.5 The two lines cross.

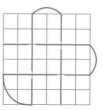

FIG 2.9 The four independent lines are joined to form a continuous motif.

to another, a continuous line is produced (see Fig 2.9). There is no rule for commencing the interweaving – the first line may be taken over or under as you choose. However, it is essential that once begun, the line is woven alternately over and under throughout the design.

Never be tempted to move to another part of the design once you have begun as there is a real danger that the interweaving will be a disaster! In complicated designs, it is often easier to commence in the middle where the straight lines cross each other.

All lines must travel straight forward at each crossing point: they do not curve or alter their direction.

Crossing point drawings for the designs given in this book can be obtained by tracing over the ribbonwork illustrated. Follow the ribbon with a single line, breaking the line where one ribbon passes under another.

Ribbonwork

Ribbons are bands of a consistent width. In all ribbonwork, the complete width of each ribbon must be shown, so where two or more ribbons pass through a space, their combined width must not be greater than the width of that space. For this reason, the width of the ribbons is determined by the smallest available space in the design. (See Plotting the Design on page 12; see also Figs 2.27–2.30.)

There are two methods for creating ribbons – both start with the basic line work drawing.

METHOD 1

The first method is to draw lines on either side of the original lines, parallel to the originals and equidistant from them. In simple patterns the crossing points can be easily identified (see Figs 2.10 and 2.11) and the ribbon can then be inked in following them. After inking the construction lines can be erased (see Figs 2.12 and 2.13).

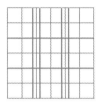

FIG 2.10 Lines are drawn either side of the original vertical lines, parallel to them.

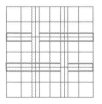

FIG 2.11 Parallel lines are drawn either side of the horizontal lines. Where these cross the vertical lines, interweaving will take place.

FIG 2.12 The horizontal ribbons are inked in following the interweaving shown in Fig 2.8.

FIG 2.13 With the vertical lines inked in the ribbonwork is complete.

METHOD 2

In more complex designs, the additional construction lines and points of intersection can be very confusing and difficult to follow. The second method for plotting ribbonwork helps to alleviate this by removing the lines at the crossing points. Rather than drawing in the new lines along the entire length of the original lines, lines on the inner side are drawn only up to the point where they meet the other new construction lines, as shown in Fig 2.15 (bordering the inside shapes), and a continuous line is drawn around the outer sides (bordering the edge). It is often simpler to complete the bordering in two or more stages, for

example, bordering the lower edge
before starting on the upper edge of the
design. As with Method 1, all the new
lines must be parallel to and equidistant
from the original lines.

Figure 2.14 shows all the additional
lines drawn in following Method 1, and
Figs 2.15–2.18 show the plotting of

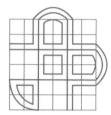

FIG **2.16** Bordering the upper edge.
Again, the outside border is half the
width of the final ribbon.

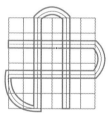

FIG **2.14** Converting Fig 2.9 to
ribbonwork following Method 1.

FIG **2.17** Bordering the lower edge.

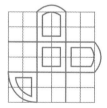

FIG **2.15** Filling in the inside shapes
following Method 2. The 'border'
around each inside shape is half the
width of the final ribbon.

FIG **2.18** The completed
ribbonwork motif.

ribbonwork following Method 2. Where the construction of ribbonwork is shown in this book, it is done following Method 2. The bordering of inside shapes and outer edges is not shown for each design for reasons of space, but the process is the same in each case and can be applied to any design.

WORKED EXAMPLES

A

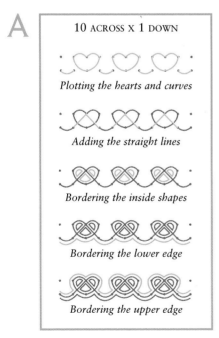

10 ACROSS X 1 DOWN

Plotting the hearts and curves

Adding the straight lines

Bordering the inside shapes

Bordering the lower edge

Bordering the upper edge

Hearts are plotted one square apart, and lines are extended from the centre of each to join the hearts into a knotted ribbon. Don't worry if your initial attempts produce a narrow ribbon – this is quite normal, and as your confidence increases, you will soon be able to regulate the width. It is sometimes an advantage to use narrow ribbons, especially at points where there is close interweaving.

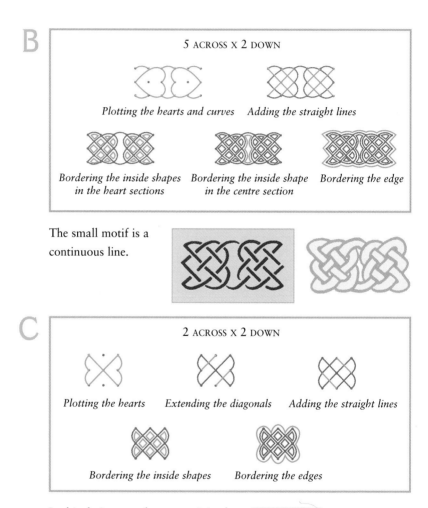

B

5 ACROSS X 2 DOWN

Plotting the hearts and curves   *Adding the straight lines*

Bordering the inside shapes   *Bordering the inside shape*   *Bordering the edge*
in the heart sections   *in the centre section*

The small motif is a continuous line.

C

2 ACROSS X 2 DOWN

Plotting the hearts   *Extending the diagonals*   *Adding the straight lines*

Bordering the inside shapes   *Bordering the edges*

In this design, two hearts are joined at the base, and the diagonal lines taken from the centre of each heart are joined to make a continuous motif.

Double ribbons

Two ribbons drawn together, each finished in a different colour, create an interesting effect. As the interweaving for double ribbons is quite complicated, initial attempts at double ribbons should be worked on large squares.

Plotting is the same as for single ribbons (plotting the line drawing and bordering the inside shapes and edges), but what would be half a ribbon for single ribbons is treated as a whole ribbon for double ribbon work, and this affects the crossing points.

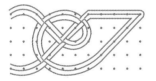

Plot and ink in the outline, then border the inside shapes and edges

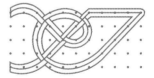

Add guidelines to indicate where the first ribbon passes under

Add guidelines to indicate where the second ribbon passes under

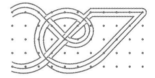

Ink in the first and then the second ribbon

Colour each ribbon

FIG 2.19 Plotting a double ribbon.

The interweaving of the first ribbon must be the opposite of that of the second; at a point where the first ribbon crosses over, the second ribbon must pass under and vice versa. Because the additional ribbon makes the interweaving more complicated, it is helpful to add guidelines to your pencil drawing to indicate where each ribbon will pass under at a crossing point. Complete the guidelines for one whole ribbon, passing alternately over and under, before starting to mark the second. Remember that whatever pattern you have chosen for the first ribbon, the pattern for the second will be the opposite.

With the interweaving indicated, ink in first one ribbon, and then the other. (See Fig 2.19.)

Split ribbon technique

By extending one or more branches from the main ribbon, the artist can weave these strands independently, before join-

The ribbon is split, one branch is interwoven, and returned to the main branch

FIG 2.20 Splitting the ribbon allows additional interweaving.

Two branches are extended from the main branch, interwoven, and rejoined in the main branch

FIG 2.21 Border frames can be created with the split ribbon technique.

ing them to the main branch again, as shown in Figs 2.20 and 2.21. This allows additional and more complicated interlacing. The technique is also very effective in creating corner motifs, as it enables the interlacing to be contained within a border frame of a suitable shape. (See Chapter 13, Corner Motifs.)

20

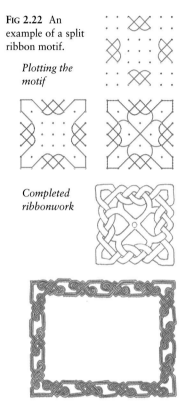

FIG 2.22 An example of a split ribbon motif.

Plotting the motif

Completed ribbonwork

FIG 2.23 A complete frame, with mitred corners.

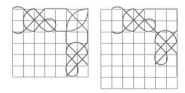

FIG 2.24 Examples of joining panels to form a mitred corner.

Mitred corners

Lengths of knotwork borders and panels can be joined at a mitred corner to form a frame (see Fig 2.23). A useful method of working out a mitred corner is as follows:

1 Draw the knot to be tested, in pencil, on graph paper.

2 On a piece of scrap graph paper draw the same knot, in ink, and cut it out. Do not leave any border around the knotwork lines.

3 Place the cut-out knot at 90° to the pencilled knot. This will show clearly the number of ends that are to be joined.

4 Try various ways of joining these ends by moving the cut-out knot nearer to, and further away from, the pencilled knot. (See Fig 2.24.)

General plotting tips

1. Use large squares to plot until you are comfortable with inter weaving, and for complex designs use 1cm squares to clarify the crossing points.

2. Placing the hearts facing towards each other produces longer side loops which can be softened by twisting.

3. Motifs can be adapted to give a border design by plotting several and joining their side loops.

4. Avoid square and pointed corners in ribbonwork unless they are required for a specific effect. Although the design is plotted using sharp corners, they should be rounded before inking in the design. (See Figs 2.25 and 2.26.)

5. Corners can be filled by adding a loop or extending a long point.

6. In patterns where a sharp corner is part of the design, round off the inside border to create a softer effect.

7. In ribbonwork, the width of the ribbon is determined by the smallest space in the design. It is essential to keep the ribbon width as uniform as possible.

8. The ends of the ribbons can be joined together.

9. When dealing with tight spaces, do not attempt to draw all the lines within the space. Instead, place a dot in the centre of the space to act as a guide. (See Figs 2.27–2.30.)

10. Plotting the hearts or loops further apart leaves more space across the centre for interweaving.

11. Complex designs can be difficult to ink in once the ribbon has been sketched. In such cases it is helpful to make a simple line drawing in a larger scale before attempting the actual working, so that the crossing points can be easily identified.

12. When a design is required to fill a specific area, divide the space into squares and select a suitable knot from any section. For example, an area of 5.5 x 2.5cm will accommodate a design requiring 11 x 5 squares, using 5mm squares. Remember to measure slightly within the area available to accommodate the outer side of the ribbon.

FIG 2.25 Rounding off the pointed corners to give a softer effect.

FIG 2.26 The softening effect of rounded corners shown in ribbonwork.

FIG 2.27 Mark the centre of the square with a dot.

FIG 2.28 Add all the inside ribbon edges.

FIG 2.29 Add all the outside ribbon edges.

FIG 2.30 The completed ribbonwork showing interweaving.

General colouring tips

1 Try out various colour combinations before embarking on the actual ribbonwork. A small heart is useful for testing colours. It is very quickly worked and has three points of interweaving which will show up different effects.
2 Try unlikely colours together for a dramatic effect.
3 Do not use colours which are very close in shade, as one tends to kill the other.

4 Be careful with dark colours and try them out first; they sometimes hide the knot and obscure the crossing points. For this reason dark colours are better with a light border on both sides of the ribbon.
5 Note carefully how many ribbons are interwoven in the selected design and work on one ribbon at a time – it is very frustrating when you find that you have coloured part of a different ribbon by mistake!

PART TWO

BASIC DESIGNS

ḃeaʀts

Hearts are created by plotting curves and straight lines. They can be adapted and embellished by extending diagonal lines from their centre, extending the base and extending the top.

✦

Hearts can be plotted in one of four ways:

a *b* *c* *d*

a

With the lower part of the heart
drawn as a semicircle

b

With the base of the heart forming
an angle of 90°

c

With a semicircular base, but plotted
diagonally (i.e. the midline of the heart runs
diagonally through the plotting square)

d

With a right-angled base,
plotted diagonally

Chapter 3

Sɑɑll ꟾᴇᴀʀᴛꜱ

All the designs in this section are constructed by plotting small hearts and extending diagonal lines from the centre of each heart to produce variations in design and interweaving.

1

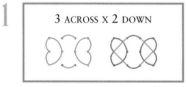

3 ACROSS X 2 DOWN

7 ACROSS X 6 DOWN

Two interwoven motifs, one a variation of Design 1. The bases are plotted three squares apart and the diagonals extended over two squares.

2

10 ACROSS X 2 DOWN

VARIATION

14 ACROSS X 5 DOWN

A variation of Design 2. Each
row of hearts is plotted two
squares apart, with a space of
three squares between the
rows. Diagonals are extended
through three squares and
interlaced.

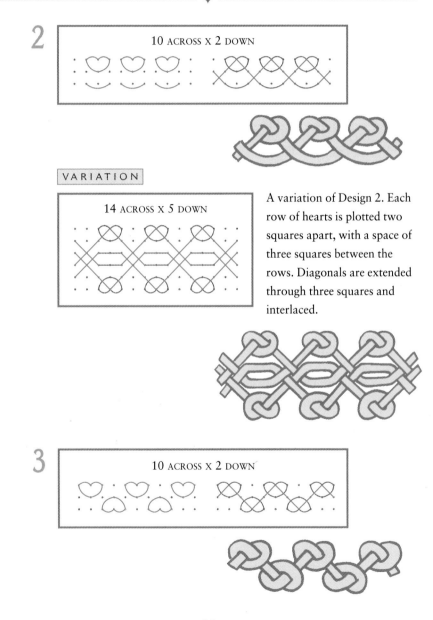

3

10 ACROSS X 2 DOWN

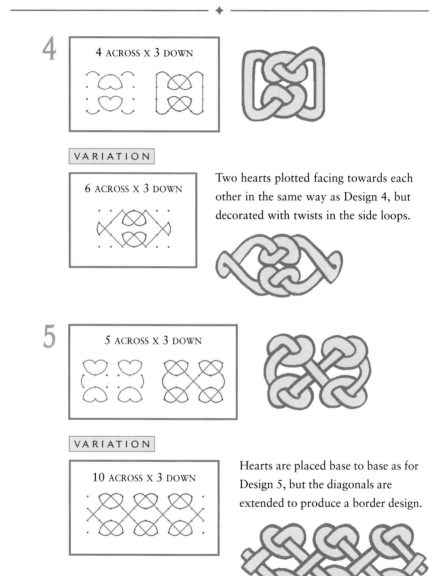

4

4 ACROSS X 3 DOWN

VARIATION

6 ACROSS X 3 DOWN

Two hearts plotted facing towards each other in the same way as Design 4, but decorated with twists in the side loops.

5

5 ACROSS X 3 DOWN

VARIATION

10 ACROSS X 3 DOWN

Hearts are placed base to base as for Design 5, but the diagonals are extended to produce a border design.

6

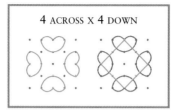

4 ACROSS X 4 DOWN

VARIATION

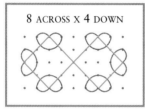

8 ACROSS X 4 DOWN

This variation of Design 6 extends parallel sides of the framework to produce a rectangular motif.

VARIATION

5 ACROSS X 5 DOWN

Another variation with the hearts plotted diagonally, and their bases pointed.

16 ACROSS X 6 DOWN

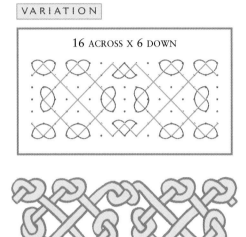

A further variation of Design 6 in which the four heart motifs are plotted further apart. This allows the long diagonals, extending from the rows of inverted hearts, to be interwoven.

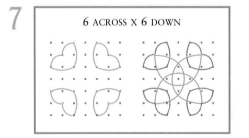

7

6 ACROSS X 6 DOWN

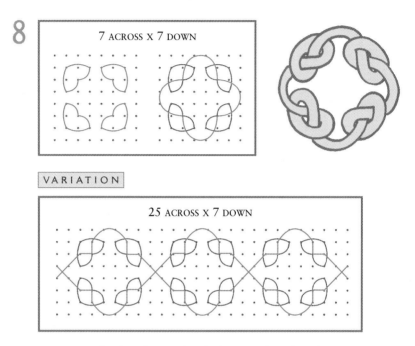

8

7 ACROSS X 7 DOWN

VARIATION

25 ACROSS X 7 DOWN

Design 8 is developed into a border by extending the sides.
Join the ends together for a continuous border.

· Sᴍᴀʟʟ Hᴇᴀʀᴛs ·

9

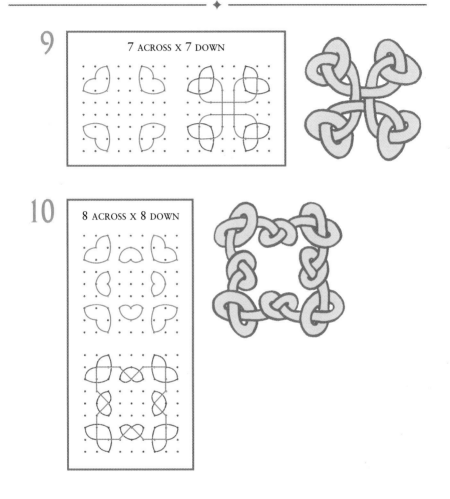

7 ACROSS X 7 DOWN

10

8 ACROSS X 8 DOWN

11

10 ACROSS X 8 DOWN

Chapter 4
Large Hearts

---------------◆---------------

Compare these designs to those in Chapter 3. They have been drawn using the same size square, but the interweaving is much tighter. For this reason, I recommend using a larger square for the initial test piece so that the crossing points and interweaving can be seen more clearly: the deeper base of the small heart allows more inter-weaving in the centre. A heart base can be plotted in one of three styles: a deep curve, a shallow curve, or pointed.

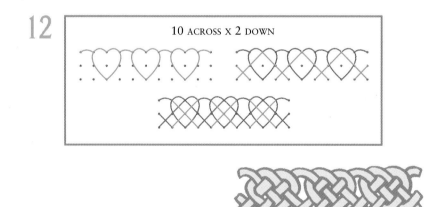

12

10 ACROSS X 2 DOWN

13

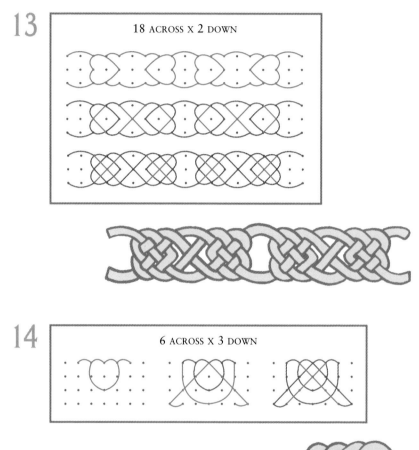

18 ACROSS X 2 DOWN

14

6 ACROSS X 3 DOWN

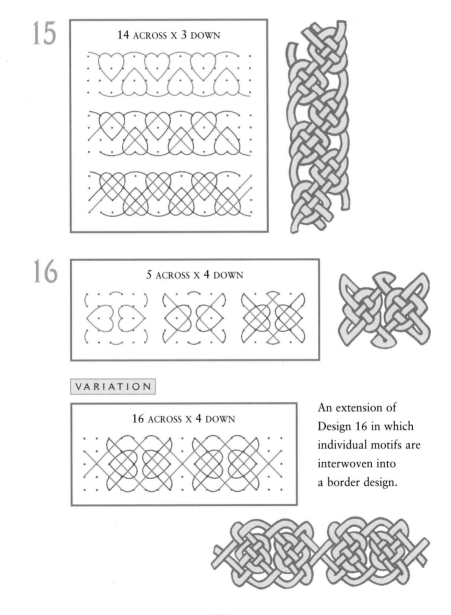

15

14 ACROSS X 3 DOWN

16

5 ACROSS X 4 DOWN

VARIATION

16 ACROSS X 4 DOWN

An extension of
Design 16 in which
individual motifs are
interwoven into
a border design.

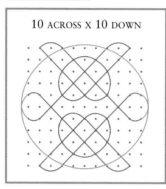

10 ACROSS X 10 DOWN

In this variation, as an alternative to twisting the diagonals together, they are interlaced and taken round the base of each heart in a semicircle.

17

7 ACROSS X 4 DOWN

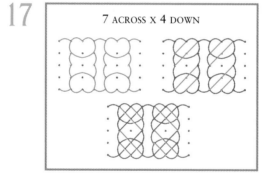

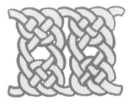

18

6 ACROSS X 5 DOWN

19

8 ACROSS X 5 DOWN

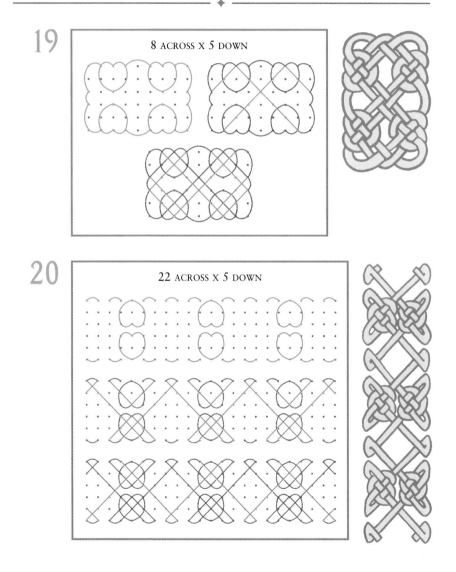

20

22 ACROSS X 5 DOWN

21

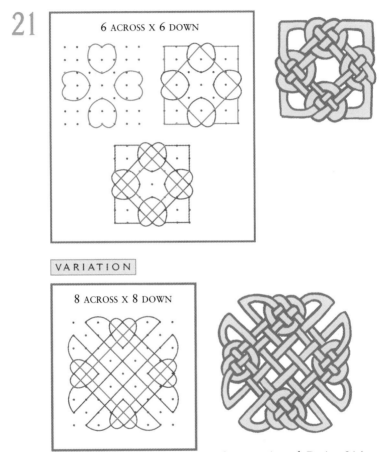

6 ACROSS X 6 DOWN

VARIATION

8 ACROSS X 8 DOWN

An extension of Design 21 in which the hearts are interwoven with four links.

· LARGE HEARTS ·

22

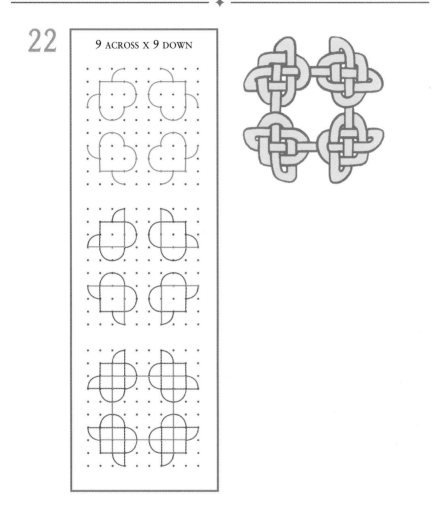

9 ACROSS X 9 DOWN

Chapter 5

EXTENDING THE BASE

In this section, the heart is plotted with a pointed base which is then extended to provide two extra diagonals. Connecting the bases of hearts reduces the length of the diagonals and side loops. Interweaving becomes tighter and although the squares are the same size as in previous sections, the designs appear smaller.

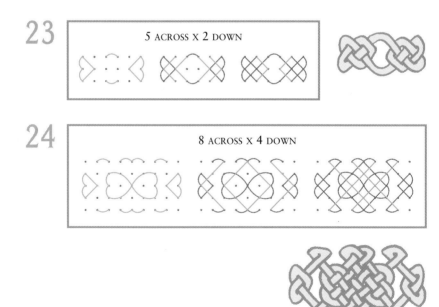

23

5 ACROSS X 2 DOWN

24

8 ACROSS X 4 DOWN

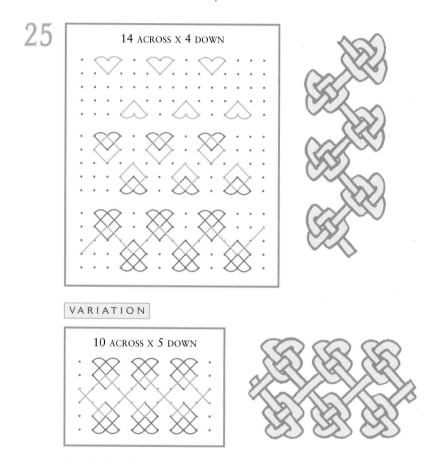

25

14 ACROSS X 4 DOWN

VARIATION

10 ACROSS X 5 DOWN

A variation of Design 25. Join the ends
together for a continuous ribbon.

26

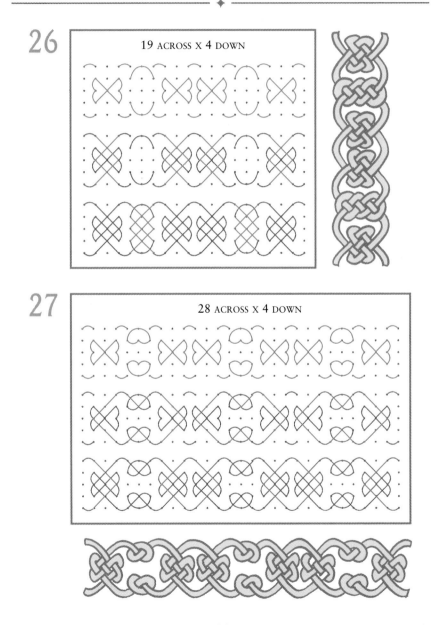

19 ACROSS X 4 DOWN

27

28 ACROSS X 4 DOWN

--- ◆ ---

VARIATION

14 ACROSS X 8 DOWN

A variation of Design 27 in which individual motifs are laced together to form a border design.

28

6 ACROSS X 6 DOWN

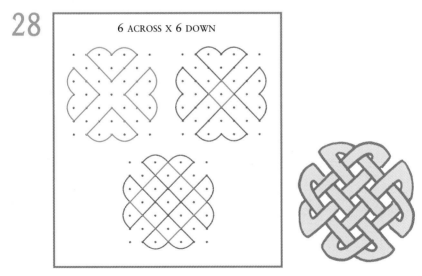

· CELTIC KNOTWORK HANDBOOK ·

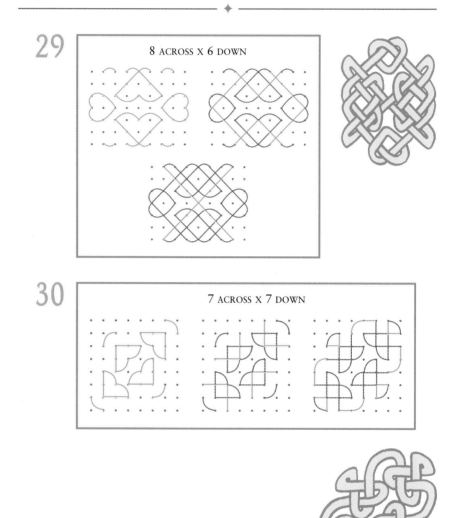

29 8 ACROSS X 6 DOWN

30 7 ACROSS X 7 DOWN

31

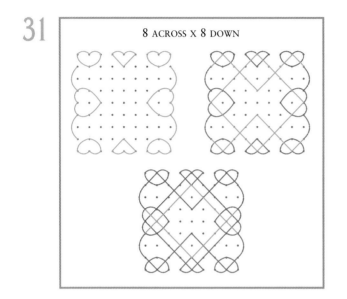

8 ACROSS X 8 DOWN

Chapter 6

EXTENDING THE TOP

Many of the designs produced by extending the top of the heart are individual woven links. The squares remain the same size, but the additional interweaving around the outside of the designs makes them appear larger.

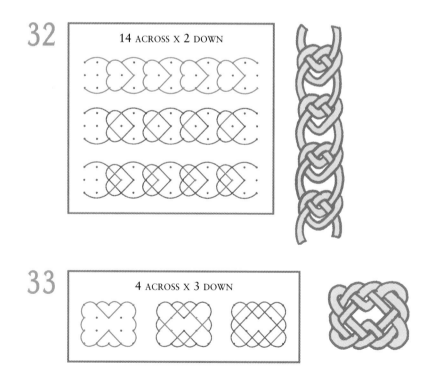

32   14 ACROSS X 2 DOWN

33   4 ACROSS X 3 DOWN

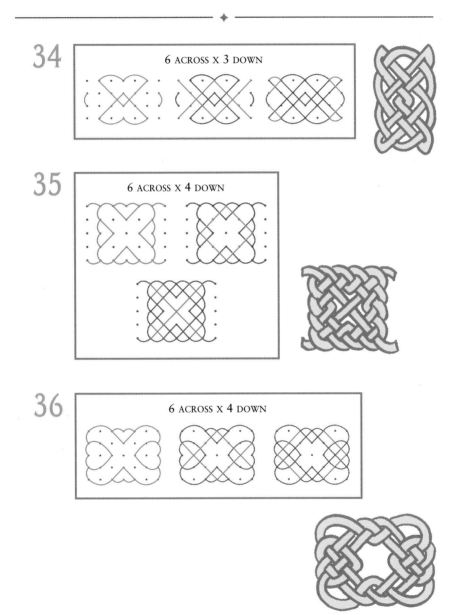

34

6 ACROSS X 3 DOWN

35

6 ACROSS X 4 DOWN

36

6 ACROSS X 4 DOWN

37

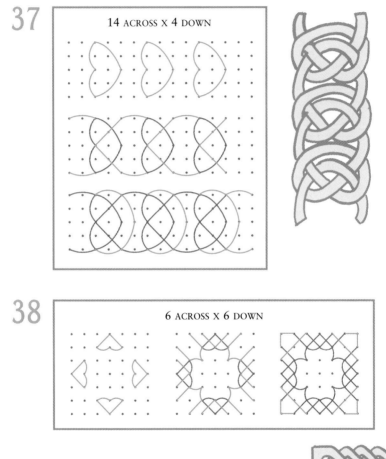

14 ACROSS X 4 DOWN

38

6 ACROSS X 6 DOWN

39

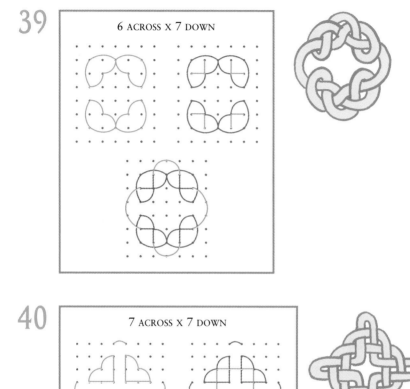

6 ACROSS X 7 DOWN

40

7 ACROSS X 7 DOWN

41

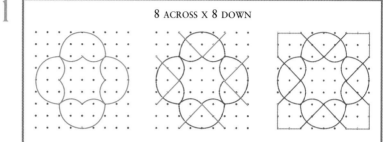

8 ACROSS X 8 DOWN

42

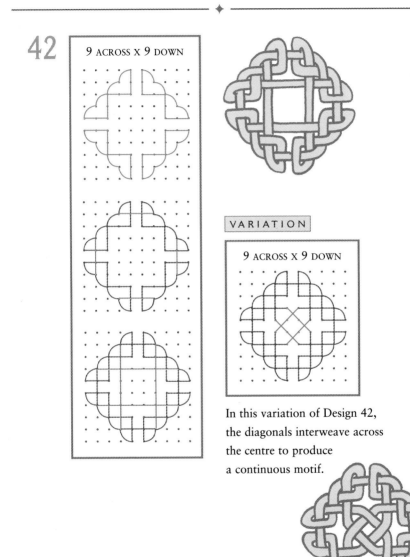

9 ACROSS X 9 DOWN

VARIATION

9 ACROSS X 9 DOWN

In this variation of Design 42,
the diagonals interweave across
the centre to produce
a continuous motif.

Chapter 7

EXTENDING THE BASE & TOP

This is the final section developed from the heart. Lines are extended from the centre, top and base to provide more ribbons for interlacing. As there are so many crossing points in the ribbons, ensure that the test piece is plotted on large squares so that these points are clear and the design can be followed through correctly.

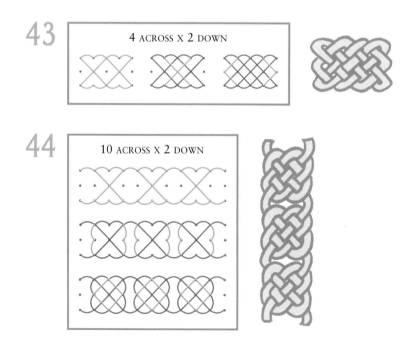

43 4 ACROSS X 2 DOWN

44 10 ACROSS X 2 DOWN

VARIATION

10 ACROSS X 8 DOWN

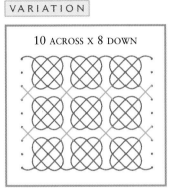

An extension of Design 44 in which the small motifs are linked into a larger panel.

45

10 ACROSS X 3 DOWN

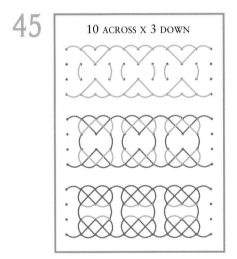

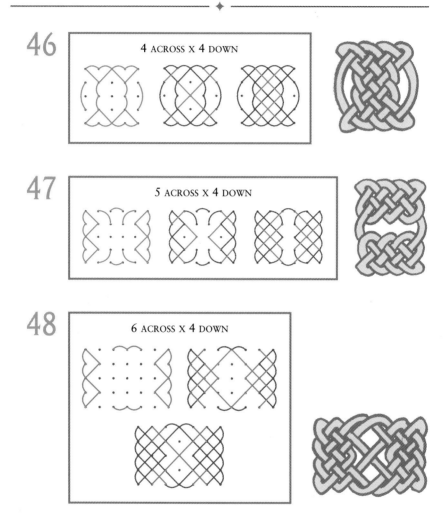

46

4 ACROSS X 4 DOWN

47

5 ACROSS X 4 DOWN

48

6 ACROSS X 4 DOWN

VARIATION

6 ACROSS X 4 DOWN

A variation of Design 48 in which hearts are plotted in the same way, but the diagonals do not cross in the centre. The motif is continuous.

49

6 ACROSS X 4 DOWN

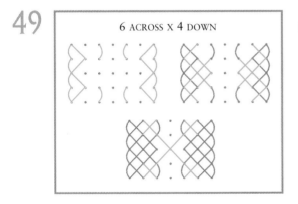

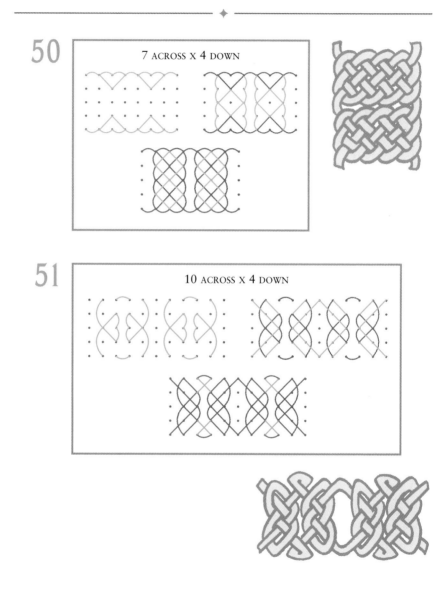

50 7 ACROSS X 4 DOWN

51 10 ACROSS X 4 DOWN

52

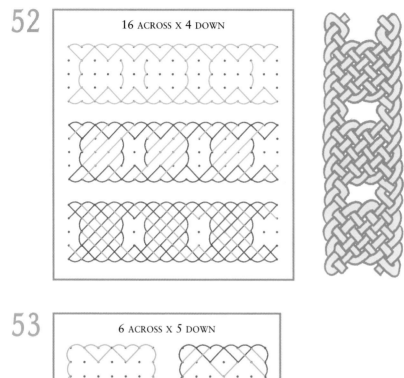

16 ACROSS X 4 DOWN

53

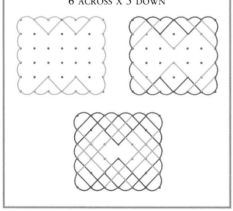

6 ACROSS X 5 DOWN

54

6 ACROSS X 6 DOWN

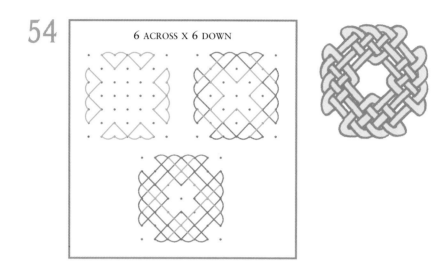

55

11 ACROSS X 11 DOWN

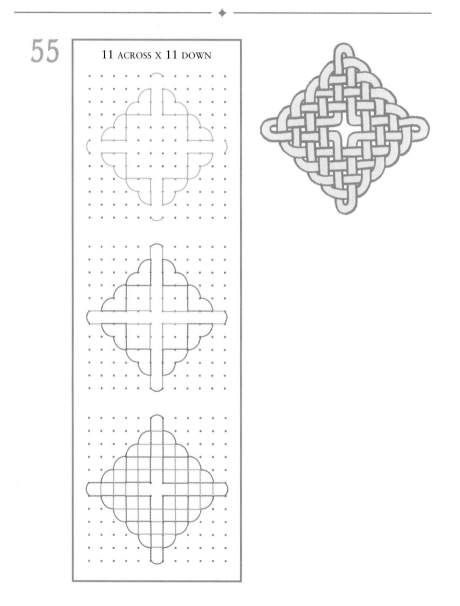

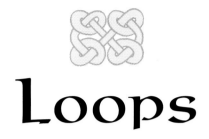

Loops

The loop is a variation of a heart – half the top remains, but the other half is free to travel in any direction, opening up greater possibilities for designs, particularly with borders.

There are four ways of plotting loops:

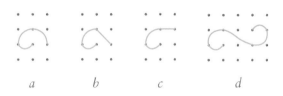

a   *b*   *c*   *d*

a
Attaching the loop to a half circle

b
Attaching one end of the loop to a quarter circle and
the other to a straight line plotted at 45° to the vertical

c
Attaching one end of the loop to a quarter circle and
the other to a straight line plotted at 90° to the vertical

d
Attaching a loop each to two quarter circles and
joining the two with a straight line

Chapter 8
Small Loops

❖

The small loop is extremely versatile: many of the designs can be combined and loose ends can be joined together in pairs. Although Design 74 is mainly straight lines, it has been included in this section as the basic plotting is worked from a small loop.

56

8 ACROSS X 2 DOWN

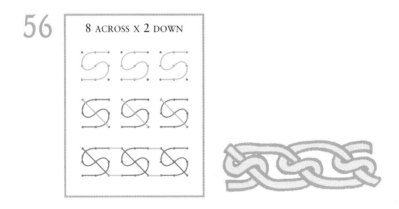

57

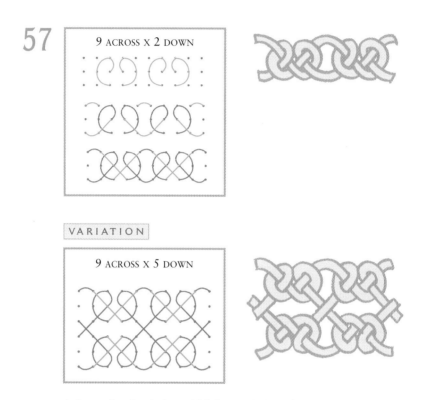

9 ACROSS X 2 DOWN

VARIATION

9 ACROSS X 5 DOWN

A deeper border design which is a variation of Design 57.
There are four ribbons in this design, the ends of which can be
joined in pairs to complete the border.

58

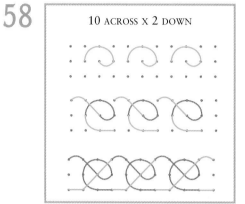

10 ACROSS X 2 DOWN

VARIATION

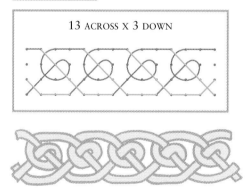

13 ACROSS X 3 DOWN

A variation of Design 58 in which the diagonals are extended to allow more interweaving between the motifs. There is a repeat of three interwoven ribbons in this continuous design.

59

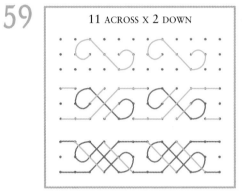

11 ACROSS X 2 DOWN

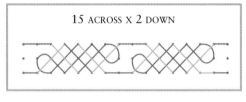

VARIATION

15 ACROSS X 2 DOWN

A variation of Design 59 in which the small loops are plotted further apart to allow more interweaving between the diagonals of each knot.

60

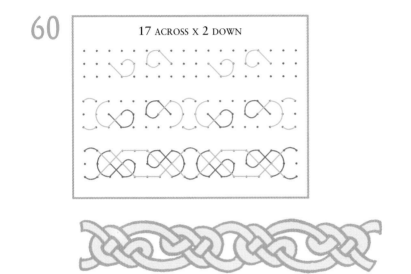

17 ACROSS X 2 DOWN

VARIATION

6 ACROSS X 6 DOWN

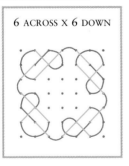

A variation of Design 60 to form a continuous motif which can be used as a frame.

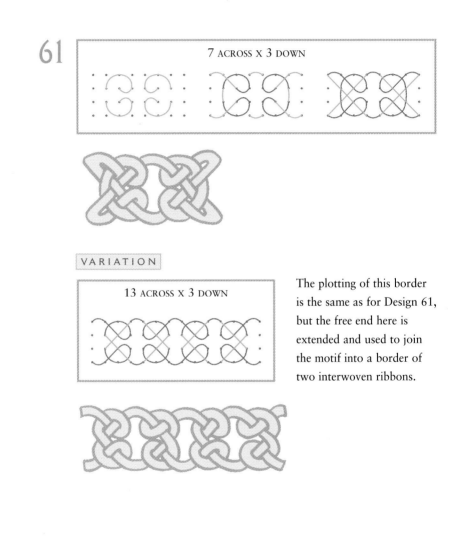

61

7 ACROSS X 3 DOWN

VARIATION

13 ACROSS X 3 DOWN

The plotting of this border
is the same as for Design 61,
but the free end here is
extended and used to join
the motif into a border of
two interwoven ribbons.

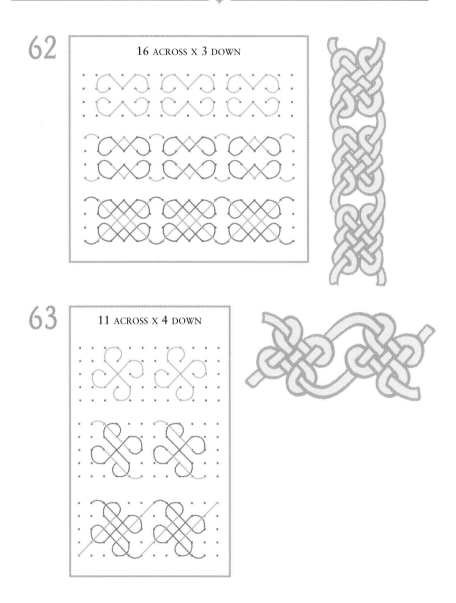

62 · 16 ACROSS X 3 DOWN

63 · 11 ACROSS X 4 DOWN

64

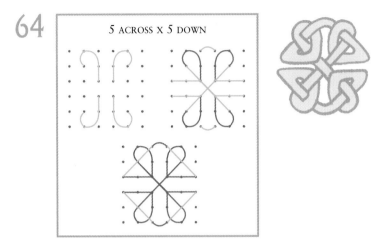

5 ACROSS X 5 DOWN

VARIATION

13 ACROSS X 5 DOWN

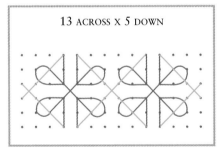

Design 64 developed into a border design. Although there are two interwoven ribbons, the ends may be joined together to make the design continuous.

· S M A L L   L O O P S ·

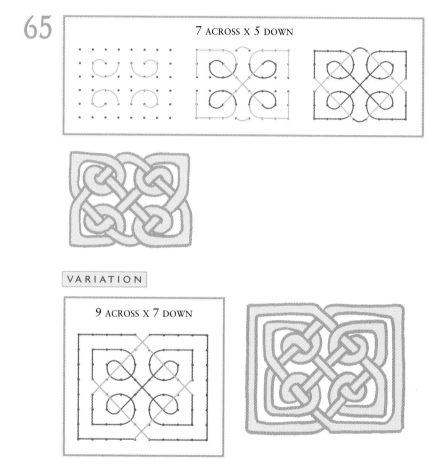

65

7 ACROSS X 5 DOWN

VARIATION

9 ACROSS X 7 DOWN

Plotted as for Design 65, the free
end of each loop is further extended
to form a double border.

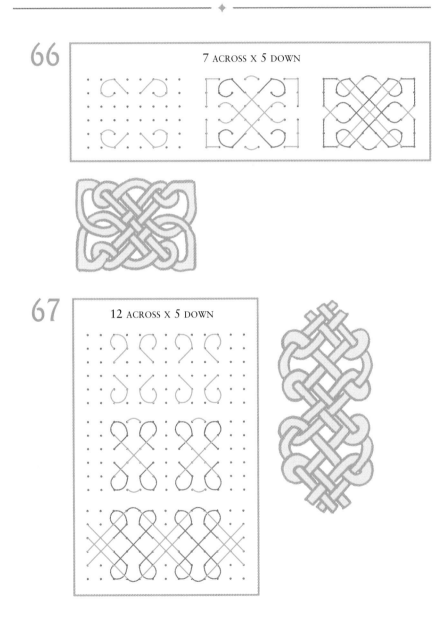

66 7 ACROSS X 5 DOWN

67 12 ACROSS X 5 DOWN

68

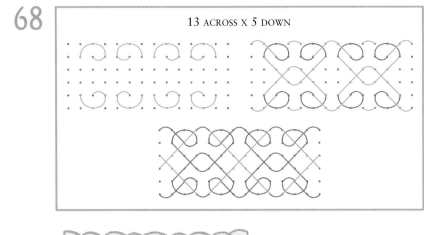

13 ACROSS X 5 DOWN

69

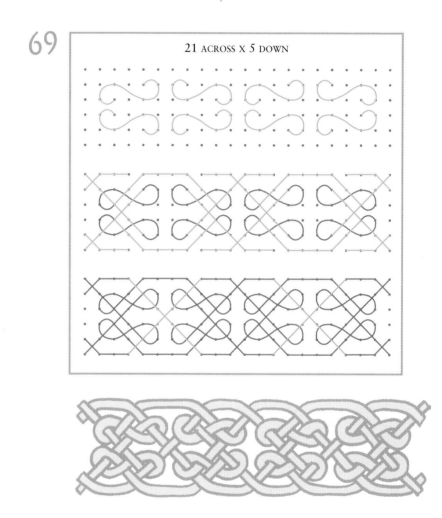

21 ACROSS X 5 DOWN

· Small Loops ·

70

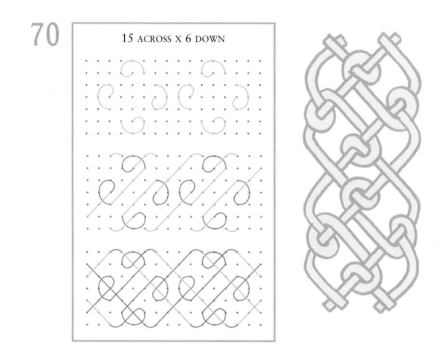

15 ACROSS X 6 DOWN

71

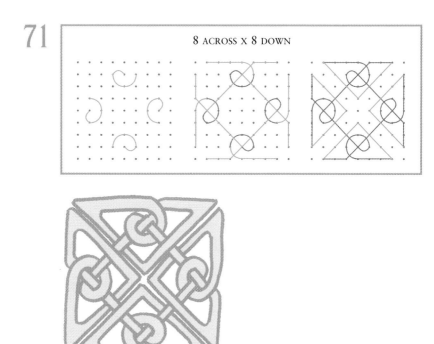

8 ACROSS X 8 DOWN

72

9 ACROSS X 9 DOWN

73

21 ACROSS X 9 DOWN

74

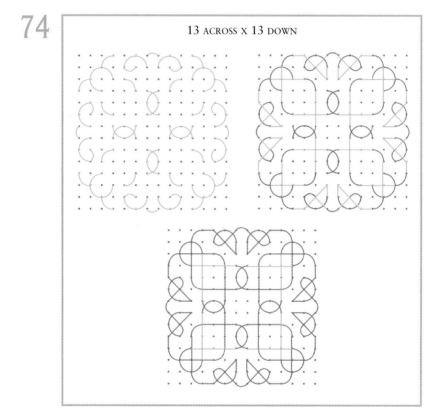

13 ACROSS X 13 DOWN

Chapter 9
LARGE LOOPS

A large loop is an extension of a small loop. This produces longer ribbons between the outer interweavings. Most large loop borders can be developed from small loops by plotting them three squares apart to allow for the extra length of ribbon. In many large loop designs a point can be introduced to add interest.

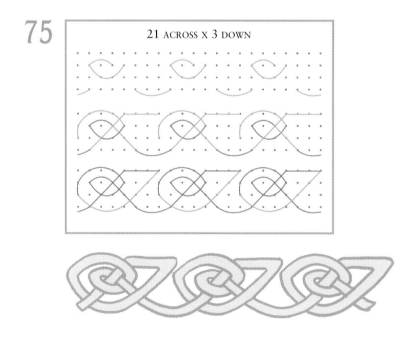

75   21 ACROSS X 3 DOWN

VARIATION

28 ᴀᴄʀᴏss x 3 ᴅᴏᴡɴ

A variation of Design 75 in which the large loops are plotted alternately down and up. The points at the outer edge turn back to interweave through the loop. The ribbon is continuous.

76

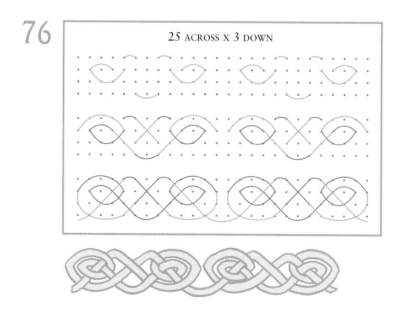

25 ᴀᴄʀᴏss x 3 ᴅᴏᴡɴ

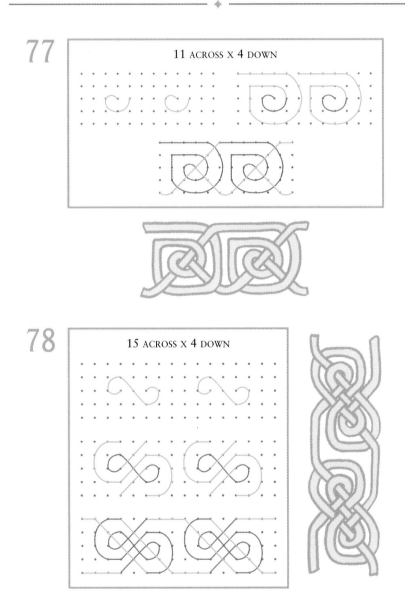

77

11 ACROSS X 4 DOWN

78

15 ACROSS X 4 DOWN

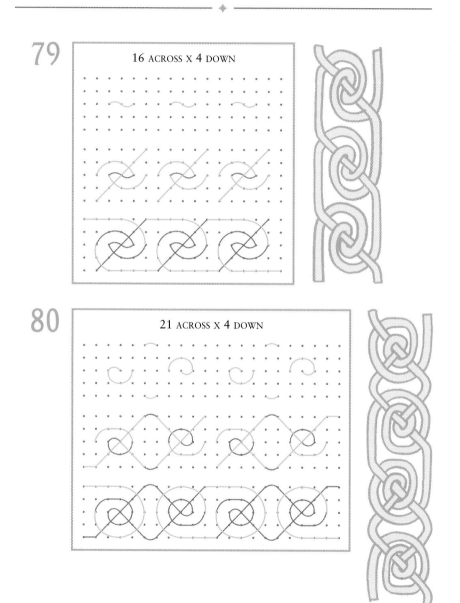

79

16 ACROSS X 4 DOWN

80

21 ACROSS X 4 DOWN

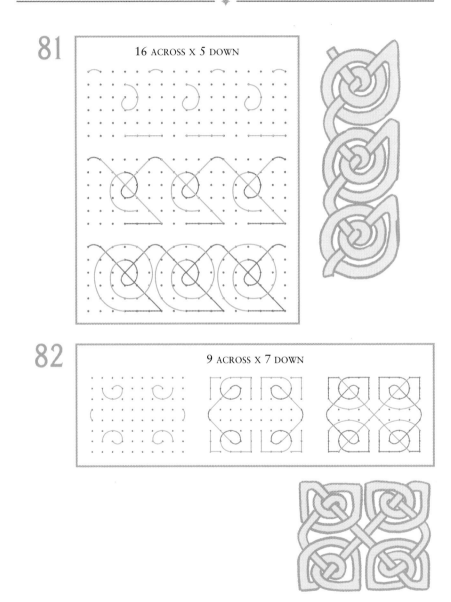

83

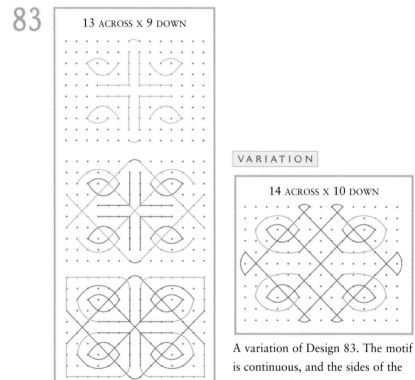

13 ACROSS X 9 DOWN

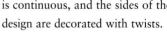

VARIATION

14 ACROSS X 10 DOWN

A variation of Design 83. The motif is continuous, and the sides of the design are decorated with twists.

84

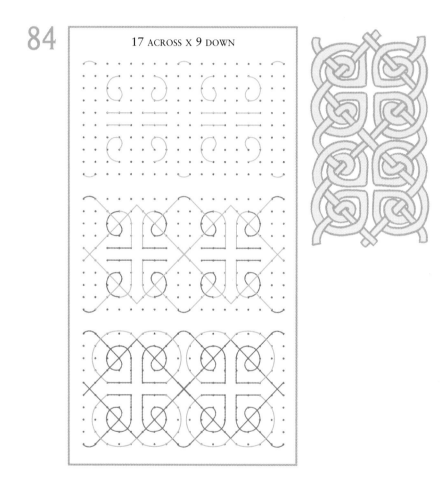

17 ACROSS X 9 DOWN

Chapter 10
Extended Loops

Extended loops are hearts which do not meet in the centre. This creates an alternative method of joining heart designs as motifs and borders: the space can either be filled with an additional curve or used to extend lines through the top of the heart.

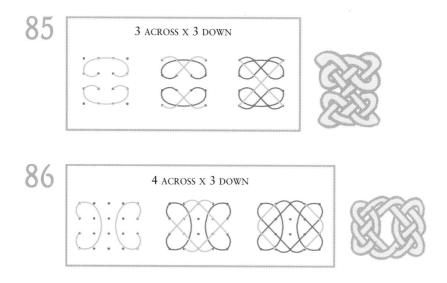

85   3 ACROSS X 3 DOWN

86   4 ACROSS X 3 DOWN

87

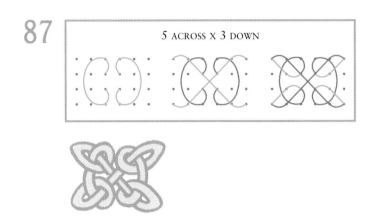

5 ACROSS X 3 DOWN

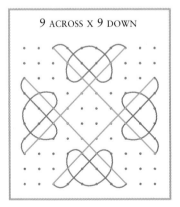

VARIATION

A variation of Design 87 in which the four loops
are plotted facing each other in a square formation.
The diagonals at the top of each loop are extended
across the square to interweave through the top of
the next loop into a continuous motif.

9 ACROSS X 9 DOWN

· Extended Loops ·

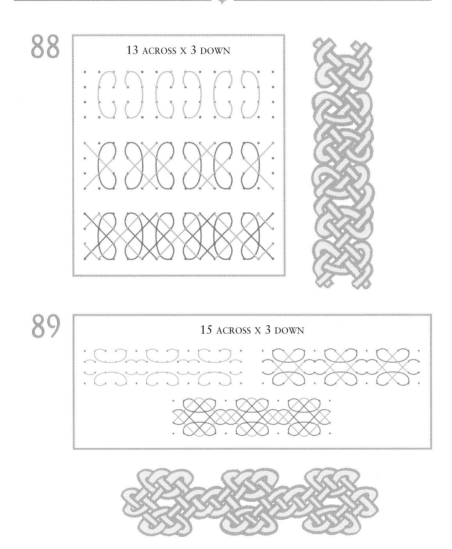

88

13 ACROSS X 3 DOWN

89

15 ACROSS X 3 DOWN

VARIATION

A variation of Design 89 to make a motif.
This motif includes a heart base extension.

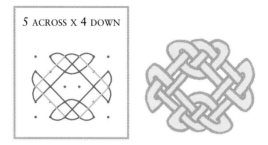

5 ACROSS X 4 DOWN

90

7 ACROSS X 5 DOWN

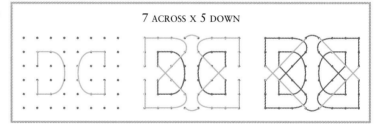

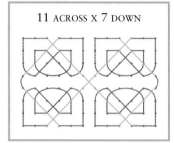

11 ACROSS X 7 DOWN

A variation of Design 90 in which the motifs are plotted one square apart and interwoven with the diagonals from the outer edge of each.

A further variation of Design 90, with angled corners.

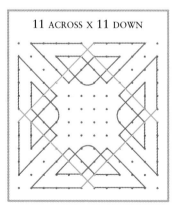

11 ACROSS X 11 DOWN

91

7 ACROSS X 5 DOWN

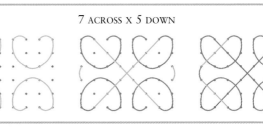

92

13 ACROSS X 5 DOWN

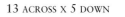

· EXTENDED LOOPS ·

93

17 ACROSS X 5 DOWN

94

21 ACROSS X 5 DOWN

95

7 ACROSS X 6 DOWN

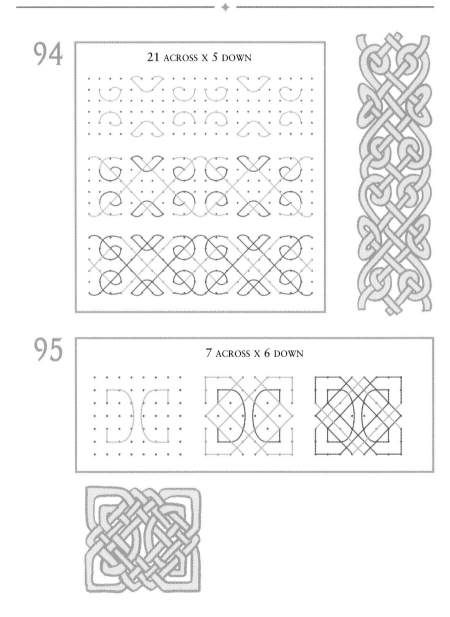

96

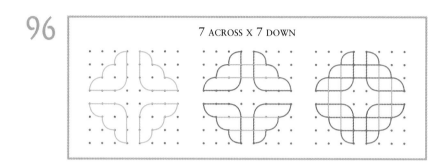

7 ACROSS X 7 DOWN

VARIATION

A variation of Design 96 in which the
sides of the four motifs are extended
outwards by one square and connected
with curves.

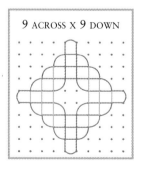

9 ACROSS X 9 DOWN

97

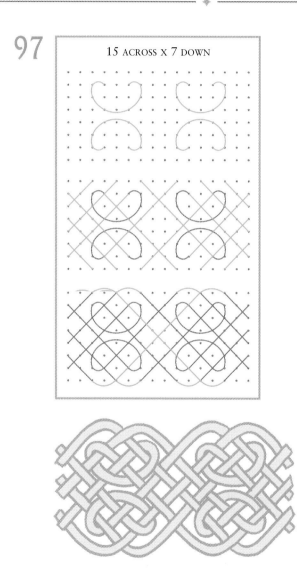

15 ACROSS X 7 DOWN

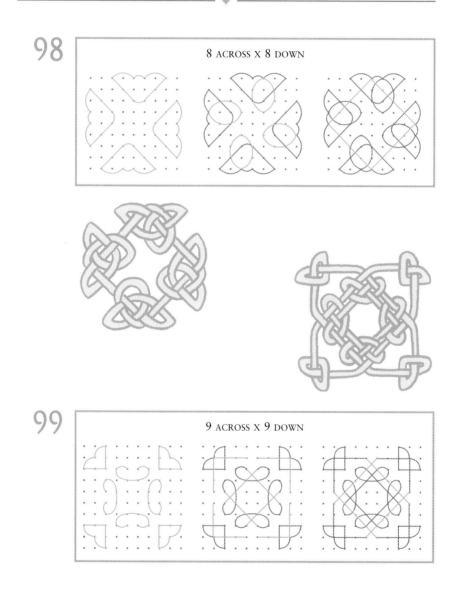

98

8 ACROSS X 8 DOWN

99

9 ACROSS X 9 DOWN

PART THREE

EXTENDING THE BASICS

Chapter 11

Combined Hearts & Loops

Combining different elements opens up design possibilities. Hearts can be combined with loops to add interest to a design and can also provide a decorative way of closing off or joining ribbons.

The designs in this section are all plotted from hearts and loops, but patterns from other sections can also be combined to develop further knotwork ribbons.

100

7 ACROSS X 2 DOWN

VARIATION

11 ACROSS X 2 DOWN

A variation of Design 100 in which pairs of small loops are plotted one square apart with loops alternately at the top and bottom. Again, the ends are decorated with small hearts.

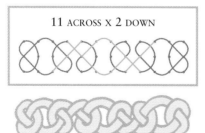

101

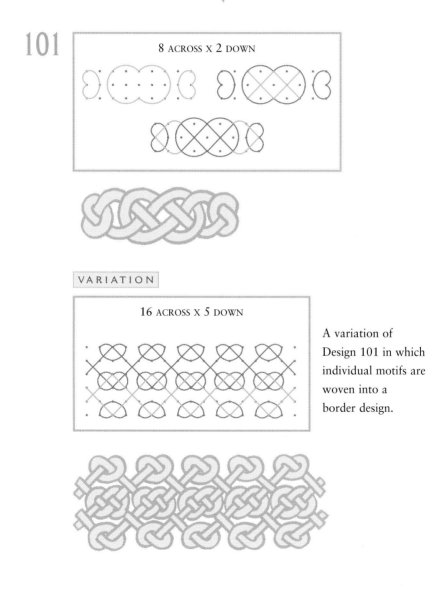

8 ACROSS X 2 DOWN

VARIATION

16 ACROSS X 5 DOWN

A variation of
Design 101 in which
individual motifs are
woven into a
border design.

102

9 ACROSS X 2 DOWN

103

12 ACROSS X 3 DOWN

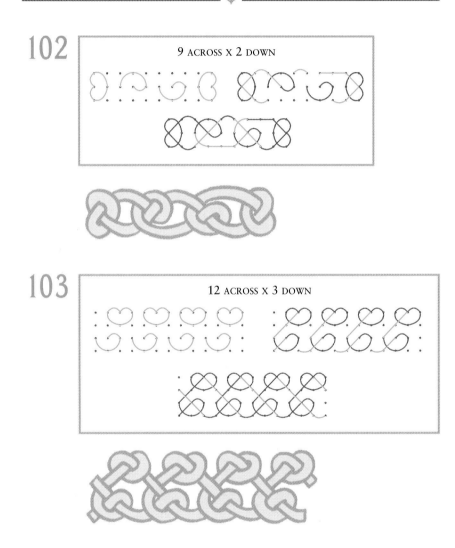

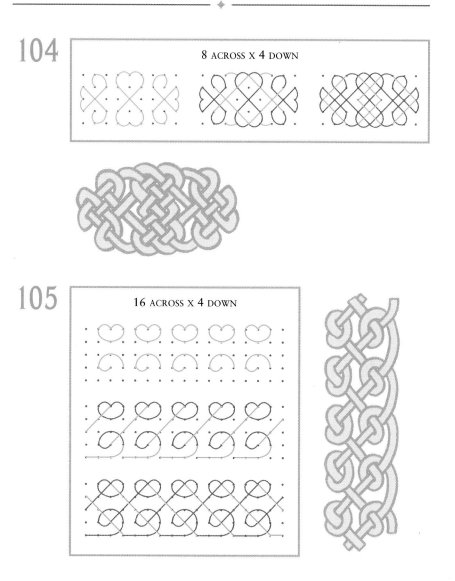

104

8 ACROSS X 4 DOWN

105

16 ACROSS X 4 DOWN

106

19 ACROSS X 4 DOWN

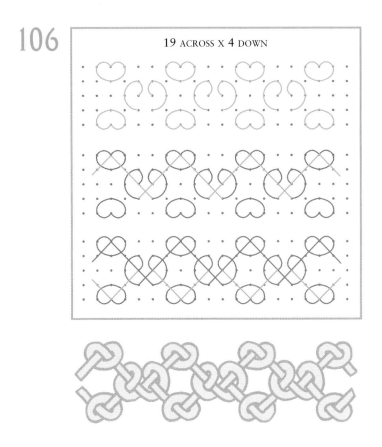

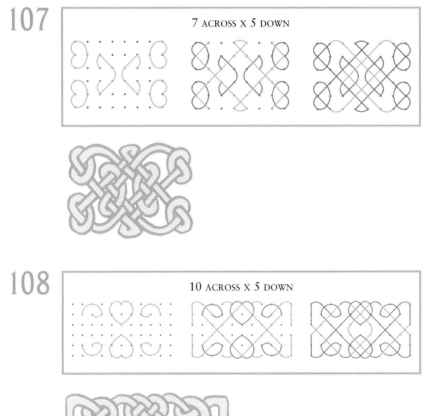

107

7 across x 5 down

108

10 across x 5 down

109

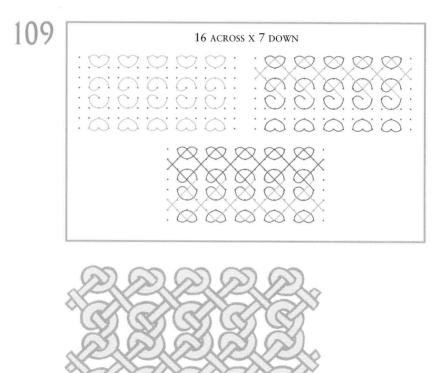

16 ACROSS X 7 DOWN

110

19 ACROSS X 7 DOWN

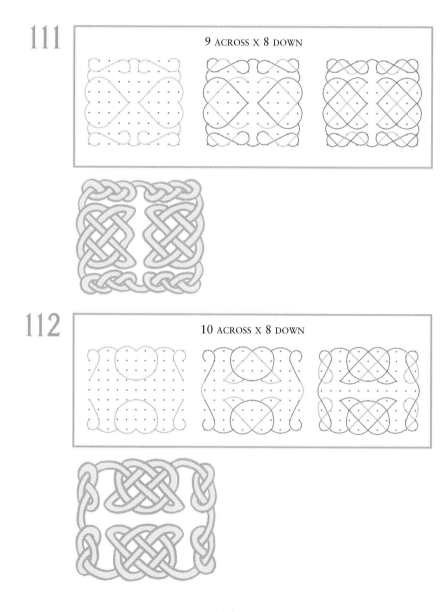

111   9 ACROSS X 8 DOWN

112   10 ACROSS X 8 DOWN

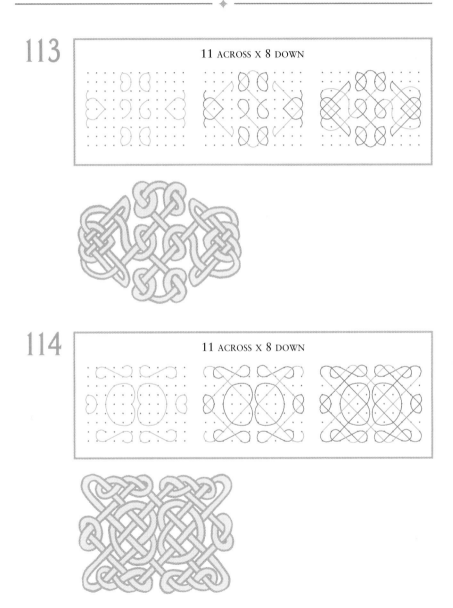

113

11 ACROSS X 8 DOWN

114

11 ACROSS X 8 DOWN

115

12 ACROSS X 9 DOWN

Chapter 12

Straight Lines

---◆---

In the previous sections the hearts or loops have been plotted first and then joined by straight lines – all the designs in this section are constructed by plotting the straight lines first.

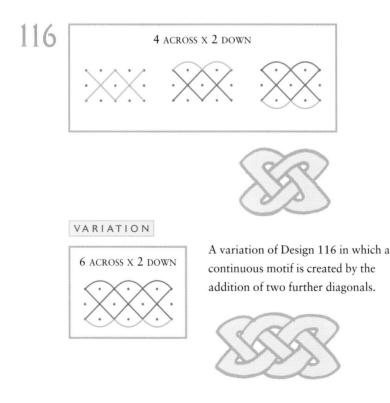

116

4 ACROSS X 2 DOWN

VARIATION

6 ACROSS X 2 DOWN

A variation of Design 116 in which a continuous motif is created by the addition of two further diagonals.

117

7 ACROSS X 2 DOWN

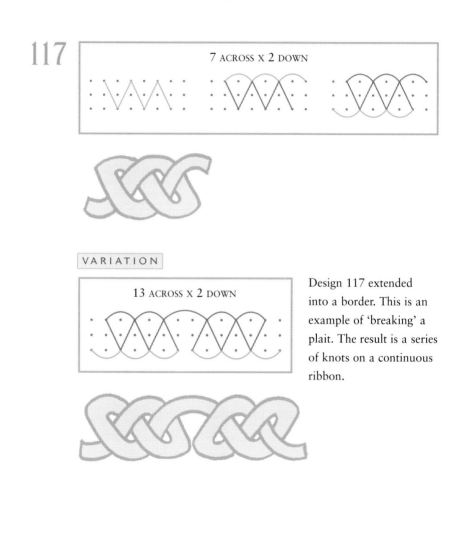

VARIATION

13 ACROSS X 2 DOWN

Design 117 extended into a border. This is an example of 'breaking' a plait. The result is a series of knots on a continuous ribbon.

118

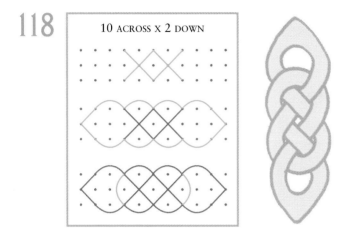

10 ACROSS X 2 DOWN

VARIATION

In this variation, Design 118 has
been extended into a border in which
individual motifs interweave.

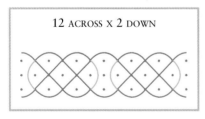

12 ACROSS X 2 DOWN

119

14 ACROSS X 2 DOWN

120

17 ACROSS X 2 DOWN

121

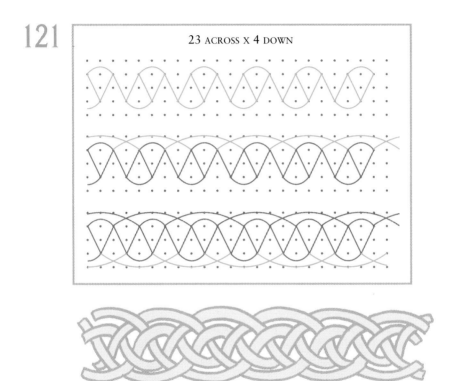

23 ACROSS X 4 DOWN

122

8 ACROSS X 6 DOWN

123

8 ACROSS X 6 DOWN

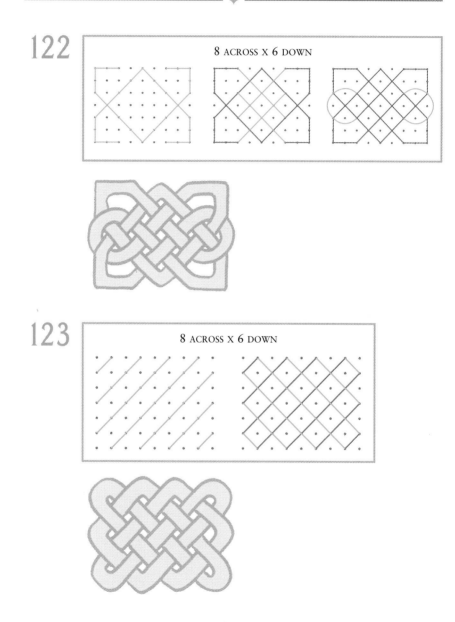

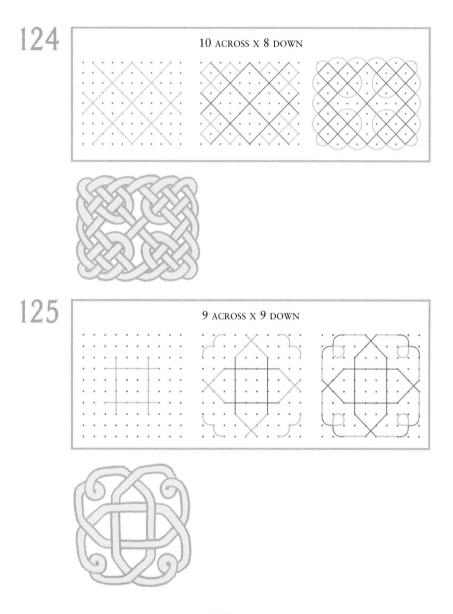

124

10 ACROSS X 8 DOWN

125

9 ACROSS X 9 DOWN

10 ACROSS X 8 DOWN

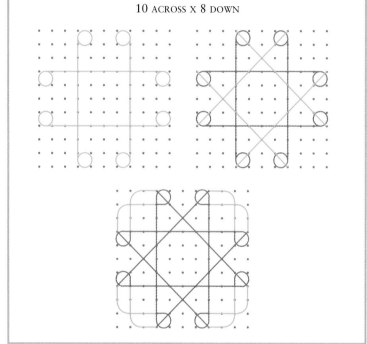

127

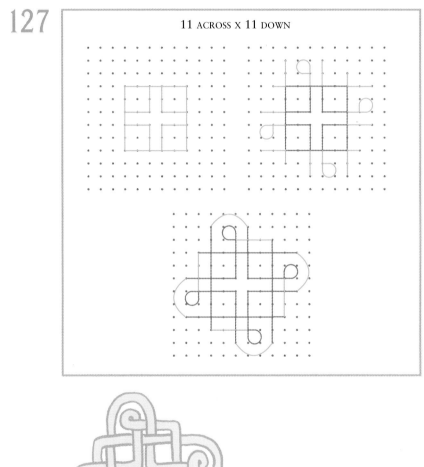

11 ACROSS X 11 DOWN

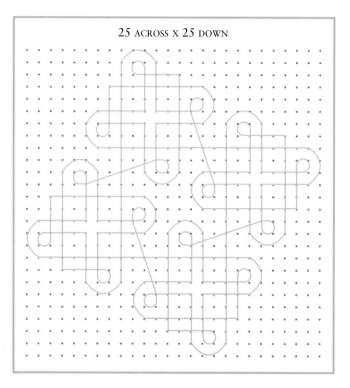

25 ACROSS X 25 DOWN

VARIATION

Design 127 arranged as a
panel. This can be extended
to cover any area. If the grid
is plotted diagonally, the
knotwork will be rotated
through 45°.

Chapter 13

CORNER MOTIFS

---◆---

Many small motifs have been included in the previous chapters for purely decorative purposes. Motifs can also be created specifically for corner designs. The split ribbon technique is very useful for this as it enables knotwork patterns to be contained within a border frame, with the whole making up one complete, single unit.

All the motifs shown here are plotted using a base from the previous chapters.

128

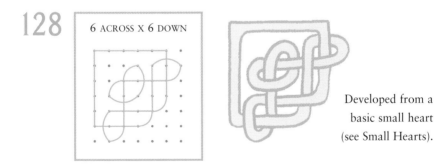

6 ACROSS X 6 DOWN

Developed from a basic small heart (see Small Hearts).

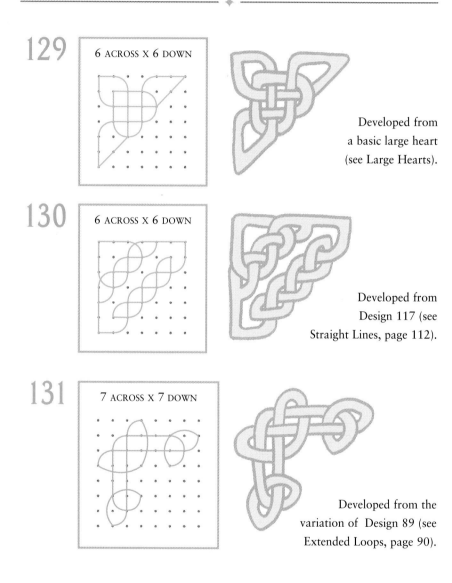

129

6 ACROSS X 6 DOWN

Developed from
a basic large heart
(see Large Hearts).

130

6 ACROSS X 6 DOWN

Developed from
Design 117 (see
Straight Lines, page 112).

131

7 ACROSS X 7 DOWN

Developed from the
variation of Design 89 (see
Extended Loops, page 90).

· CORNER MOTIFS ·

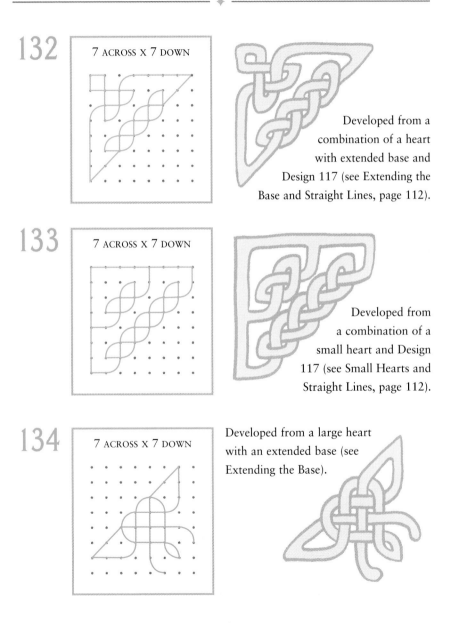

132

7 ACROSS X 7 DOWN

Developed from a combination of a heart with extended base and Design 117 (see Extending the Base and Straight Lines, page 112).

133

7 ACROSS X 7 DOWN

Developed from a combination of a small heart and Design 117 (see Small Hearts and Straight Lines, page 112).

134

7 ACROSS X 7 DOWN

Developed from a large heart with an extended base (see Extending the Base).

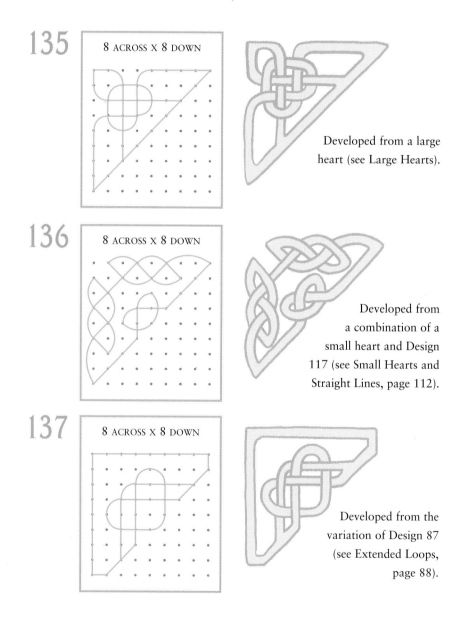

135

8 ACROSS X 8 DOWN

Developed from a large heart (see Large Hearts).

136

8 ACROSS X 8 DOWN

Developed from a combination of a small heart and Design 117 (see Small Hearts and Straight Lines, page 112).

137

8 ACROSS X 8 DOWN

Developed from the variation of Design 87 (see Extended Loops, page 88).

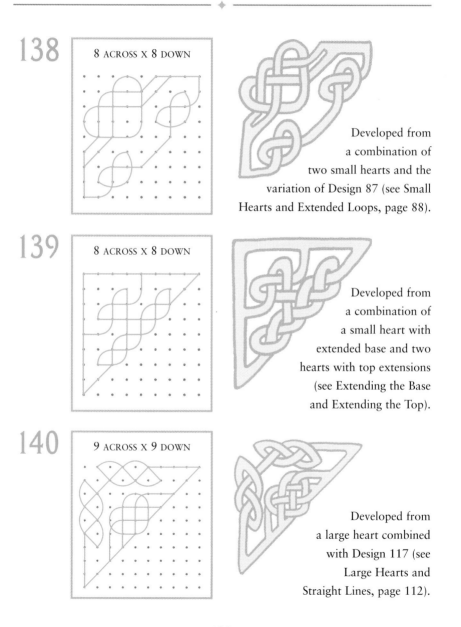

138

8 ACROSS X 8 DOWN

Developed from a combination of two small hearts and the variation of Design 87 (see Small Hearts and Extended Loops, page 88).

139

8 ACROSS X 8 DOWN

Developed from a combination of a small heart with extended base and two hearts with top extensions (see Extending the Base and Extending the Top).

140

9 ACROSS X 9 DOWN

Developed from a large heart combined with Design 117 (see Large Hearts and Straight Lines, page 112).

141

10 ACROSS X 10 DOWN

Based on an original plaitwork
design (see History,
pages 6 and 7).

142

11 ACROSS X 11 DOWN

Developed from a combination of
two small hearts with extended
bases and the variation of
Design 116 (see Extending
the Base and
Straight
Lines,
page 111).

Chapter 14

MITRED CORNERS

◆

Most continuous borders and panels can be adapted to produce decorative frames by joining two lengths at a mitred corner. There are various ways of creating mitred corners – it is simply a matter of finding a way to turn the free ends of the ribbons through 45°.

A useful method of working this out is to draw a length of the border or panel on graph paper and then cut a section out. When the cut-out section is placed at 90° to the remaining length of border, a suitable way of joining the ribbons can be found. (See Chapter 2, Materials and Techniques, page 21.)

The corners presented here have been developed from designs appearing in the earlier chapters.

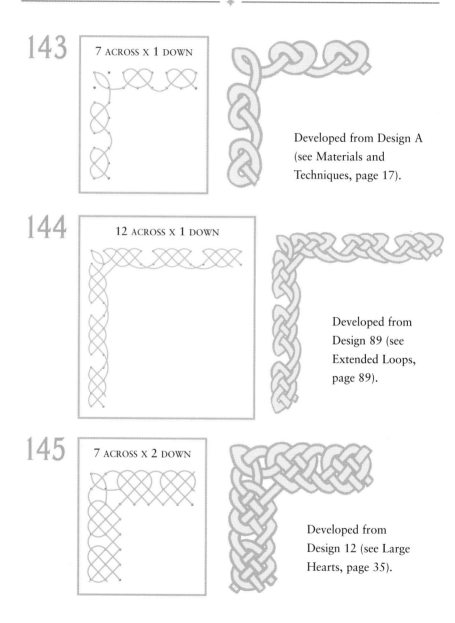

143

7 ACROSS X 1 DOWN

Developed from Design A (see Materials and Techniques, page 17).

144

12 ACROSS X 1 DOWN

Developed from Design 89 (see Extended Loops, page 89).

145

7 ACROSS X 2 DOWN

Developed from Design 12 (see Large Hearts, page 35).

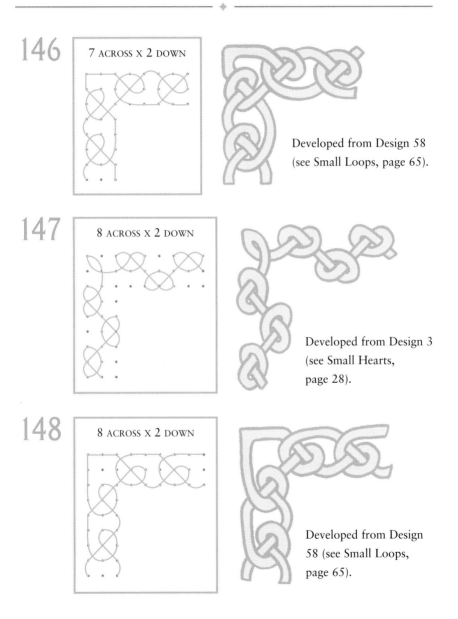

146

7 ACROSS X 2 DOWN

Developed from Design 58
(see Small Loops, page 65).

147

8 ACROSS X 2 DOWN

Developed from Design 3
(see Small Hearts,
page 28).

148

8 ACROSS X 2 DOWN

Developed from Design
58 (see Small Loops,
page 65).

149

9 ACROSS X 2 DOWN

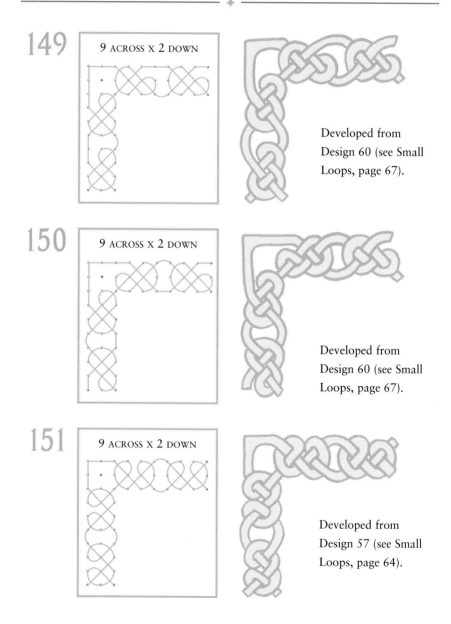

Developed from
Design 60 (see Small
Loops, page 67).

150

9 ACROSS X 2 DOWN

Developed from
Design 60 (see Small
Loops, page 67).

151

9 ACROSS X 2 DOWN

Developed from
Design 57 (see Small
Loops, page 64).

152

9 ACROSS X 2 DOWN

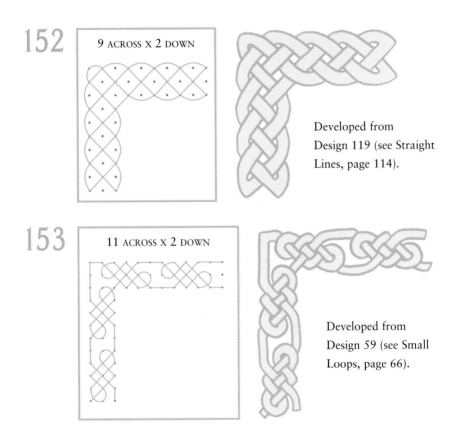

Developed from
Design 119 (see Straight
Lines, page 114).

153

11 ACROSS X 2 DOWN

Developed from
Design 59 (see Small
Loops, page 66).

154

11 ACROSS X 2 DOWN

Developed from
Design 2 (see Small
Hearts, page 28).

155

14 ACROSS X 2 DOWN

Developed from
the variation of
Design 117
(see Straight Lines,
page 112).

156

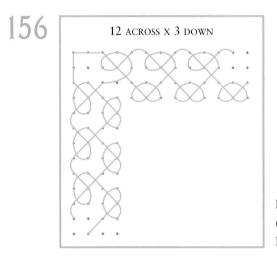

12 ACROSS X 3 DOWN

Developed from Design 109
(see Combined Hearts and
Loops, page 106).

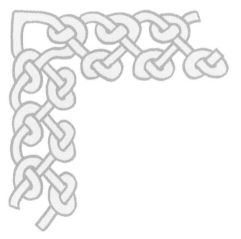

157

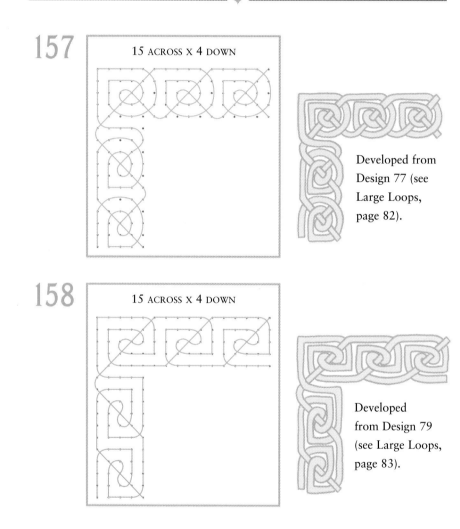

15 ACROSS X 4 DOWN

Developed from Design 77 (see Large Loops, page 82).

158

15 ACROSS X 4 DOWN

Developed from Design 79 (see Large Loops, page 83).

159

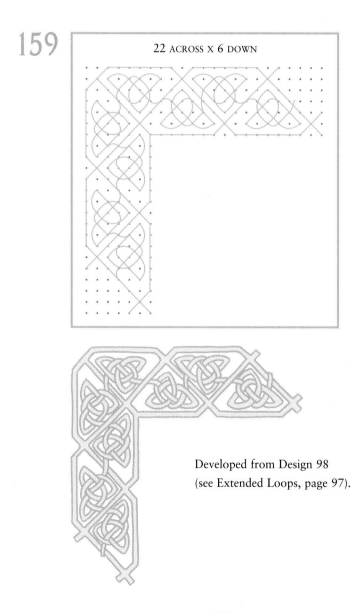

22 ACROSS X 6 DOWN

Developed from Design 98
(see Extended Loops, page 97).

Chapter 15

ZOOMORPHICS

Zoomorphic designs include animal, reptile, fish or bird motifs. Human figures are known as anthropomorphics. Heads and tails can be added to finish off the ends of knotwork borders or inserted into a point where the ribbon is not interwoven. More intricate lacing can be achieved by extending feet, eyes, ears, tails and tongues to produce further knotting. Bands of animals can be joined by allowing each creature to bite the one in front.

There are many designs composed entirely of animals, wonderful examples being the four gospels in *The Book of Kells* in which Matthew is depicted as a lion, Mark as a man (or angel), Luke as a calf, and John as an eagle.

The motifs presented here have been developed from designs included in the earlier chapters. The designs should be plotted and completed in the usual way. The next step is where the true artistic touch shows! There are no rules when filling in the bodies of animals and the leaves of plants – imagination must run freely.

160

13 ACROSS X 2 DOWN

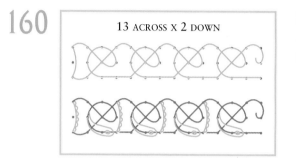

Developed from Design 58 (see Small Loops, page 65).

161

8 ACROSS X 3 DOWN

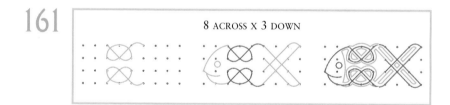

Developed from Design 4 (see Small Hearts, page 29).

162

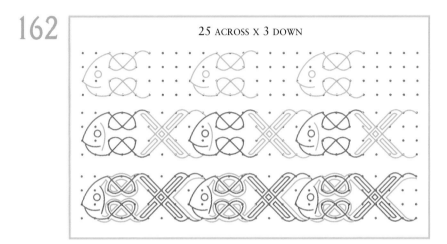

25 ACROSS X 3 DOWN

Developed from Design 4 (see Small Hearts, page 29).

163

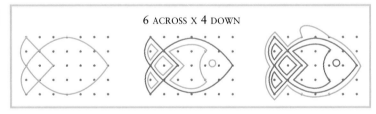

6 ACROSS X 4 DOWN

A small heart with a right-angled
base developed into a motif.

164

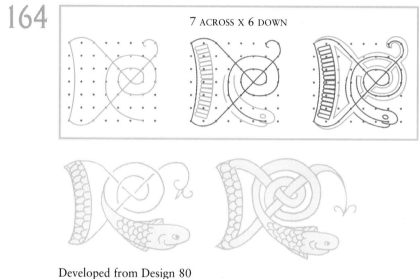

7 ACROSS X 6 DOWN

Developed from Design 80
(see Large Loops, page 81).

165

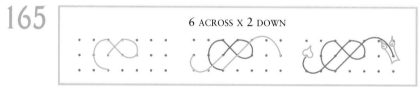

6 ACROSS X 2 DOWN

Developed from Design 60
(see Small Loops, page 67).

166

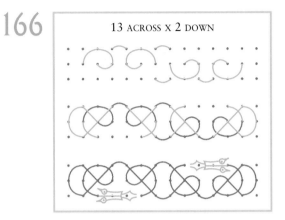

13 ACROSS X 2 DOWN

Developed from a base of small loops.

167

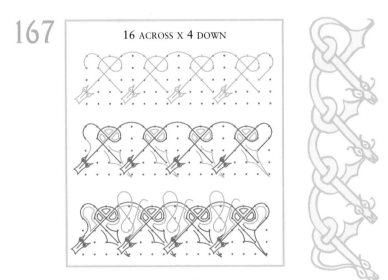

16 ACROSS X 4 DOWN

Developed from Design 58
(see Small Loops, page 65).

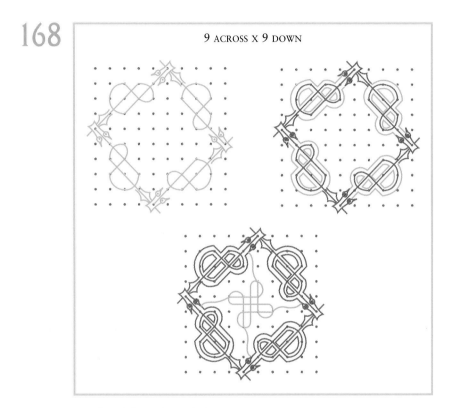

168

9 ACROSS X 9 DOWN

Developed from the variation
of Design 60 and Design 67
(see Small Loops, pages 63
and 69).

169

10 ACROSS X 10 DOWN

Developed from Design 118
(see Straight Lines, page 113).

170

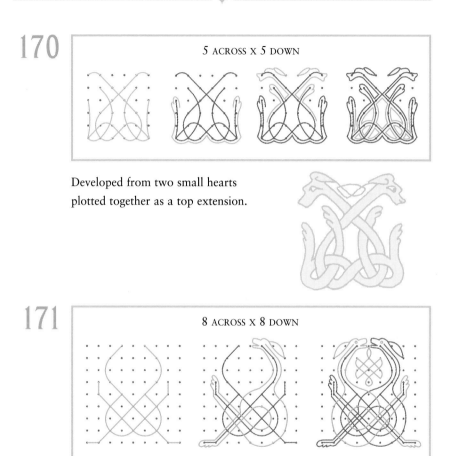

5 ACROSS X 5 DOWN

Developed from two small hearts
plotted together as a top extension.

171

8 ACROSS X 8 DOWN

Based on the large heart. Note that the
pointed heart top is not used in the motif.

172

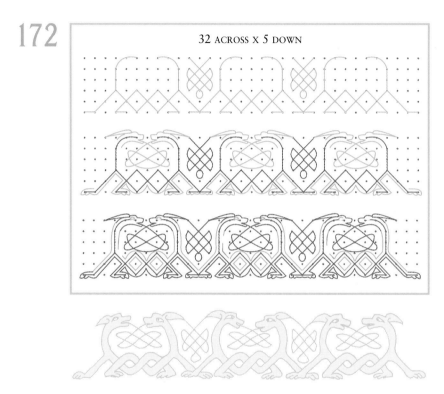

32 ACROSS X 5 DOWN

Developed from Designs C, 85 and
116 (see Materials & Techniques,
Extended Loops and Straight Lines,
pages 18, 87 and 111).

173

17 ACROSS X 6 DOWN

Bird motif using a large heart and interweaving four necks.

174

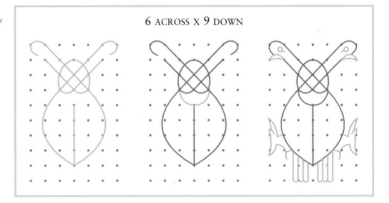

6 ACROSS X 9 DOWN

This motif uses a large heart
to interweave the necks.

175

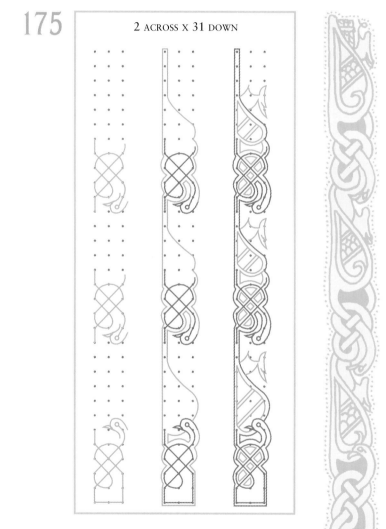

2 ACROSS X 31 DOWN

Developed from Design 60
(see Small Loops, page 67).

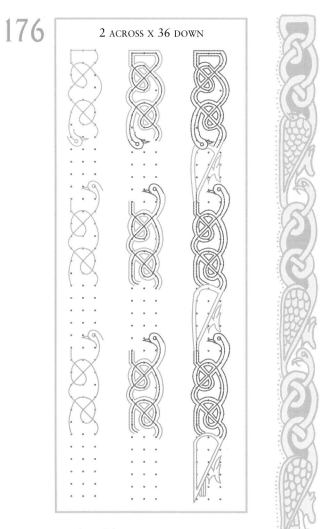

176

2 ACROSS X 36 DOWN

Developed from Design 58
(see Small Loops, page 65).

177

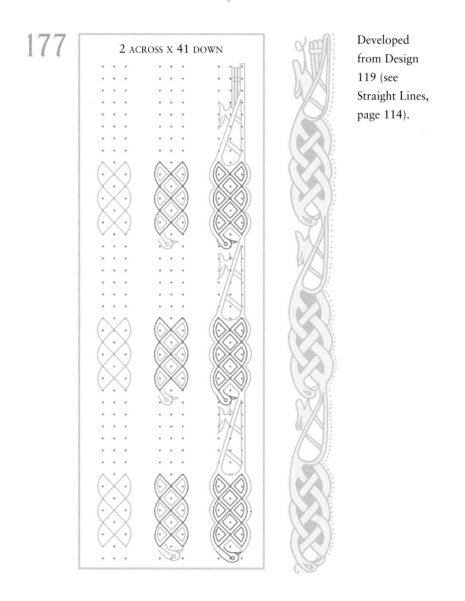

2 ACROSS X 41 DOWN

Developed
from Design
119 (see
Straight Lines,
page 114).

178

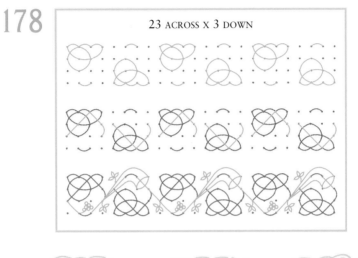

23 ACROSS X 3 DOWN

Developed from Design 98
(see Extended Loops, page 97).

179

13 ACROSS X 5 DOWN

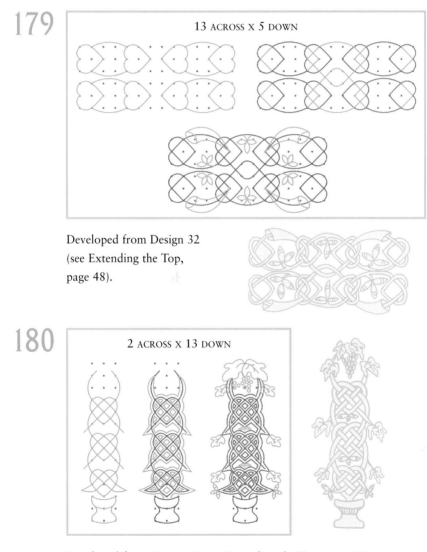

Developed from Design 32
(see Extending the Top,
page 48).

180

2 ACROSS X 13 DOWN

Developed from Design 32 (see Extending the Top, page 48).

Chapter 16

CREATING YOUR OWN DESIGNS

Excellent knotwork can be achieved by tracing or copying designs, but creating your own gives you the freedom to combine, adapt and plot designs to suit exact requirements.

The initial difficulty when attempting knotwork is understanding how the ribbons interweave, but confidence is gained with practice. The method in this book is reliable and simple and can be applied to any knotwork design.

Once the principles of this method are understood, you can experiment with plotting shapes in different positions and try alternative ways of extending, embellishing and joining them.

Try drawing hearts or loops over a sheet of paper and joining them in

different ways by extending lines from each. Varying the placement of the hearts and loops will produce different designs, and modifying their basic shape will open up the possibilities still more.

Grids

The designs in this book were all plotted on a regular grid, but even this can be modified, and as the grid influences the outline of the final design, this gives you the freedom to fill all kinds of shapes.

Throughout the book the designs have been plotted on square or rectangular grids, and these grids have been measured in terms of the number of squares across and the number of squares down. When grids are modified to fit other shapes, these 'squares' become distorted so that they are no longer true squares. To avoid confusion, I have referred to 'squares' in modified grids as divisions.

Circular and other geometric designs

As for squares and rectangles, the space to be filled must be marked into the number of divisions required to fit the chosen design. However, with circular grids these divisions will not be squares, and will not be of a uniform size: they become narrower as they move towards the centre of the circle and wider as they move away from it.

Translating the design to a circular grid, the number of divisions across equates with the number of divisions around the circumference of the circle, and these are marked out using a protractor. For example, a design that fills four divisions across will require a total

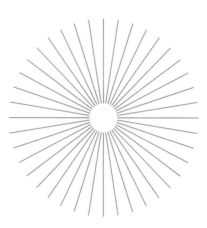

FIG 16.1 Marking out the divisions 'across' for a circular design.

number of divisions that is divisible by four. If nine repeats of the design are desired, 36 divisions will be required. The angle at which to mark out each division is found by dividing 360°, the circumference of the circle, by the number of divisions there will be. In this example the angle required is 10° (360° ÷ 36), so lines extending out from a central point are drawn at angles of 10° from each other. (See Fig 16.1.)

The number of divisions down is marked out by scribing concentric and equidistant circles over these lines. The number of circles that need to be scribed is one more than the number of divisions required. In Fig 16.2, two divisions down are required so three concentric circles have been scribed.

(the bigger the radius, the bigger the design); these should be set accordingly. For a pattern with several divisions, the centre row will be the closest to regular squares – those above will be wider and those below narrower.

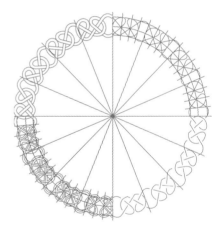

FIG 16.3 Various stages in the completion of a circular design.

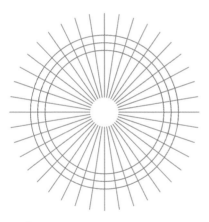

FIG 16.2 Equidistant circles are scribed to mark the divisions 'down'.

The actual size of each division, and thus of the motifs in the design, is determined by the radii of the circles scribed

The same method is used for drafting designs to fit other geometric shapes, such as hexagons and pentagons – the 'circumference' is adjusted to fit the outline of the particular shape.

Irregular shapes

Grids can be adapted to fill any size or
shape. It is not really necessary to use a
grid, but it does help if the irregular
shape is to be mirrored in another part of
the design, for example, in each corner.
Irregular grids are simple to construct.
Divisions are used as for a regular grid
and marked over the shape, across and
down, but are drawn to conform to the
shape. This means that the grid produced
is not composed of regular, square
divisions and the knots produced will not
be uniform (see Fig 16.4). A typical
example is a small heart which has half
of its top extended over two or more
divisions.

FIG 16.4 Plotting on
an irregular grid to fill
an irregular shape.

Substituting an outline
with a knot

To substitute a knot for an outline, trace
the outline of the shape and select or
create a knot. The design used for the
fish in Figs 16.5–16.7 was Design 62 (see

FIG 16.5 A knot is substituted for the
outline, but the original fin is retained.

Small Loops, page 69). Mark a grid
within the outline – this may be regular
or irregular as required – and plot the
design in the usual way. The whole outline can be included in the knot, or some
parts kept as for the original design.

The examples of fish, shown here,
demonstrate the method. The knot in
Fig 16.5 shows the fins kept as part of

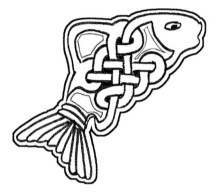

Fig 16.6 The same design as Fig 16.5, but with the fin included as part of the knot.

the original outline, while the knots in Figs 16.6 and 16.7 show them included as part of the ribbon. This is done following the zoomorphic method of extending ribbons to form limbs, tongues and tails.

Embellishment

For a more decorative border or motif, two or more knots may be combined in the one design. For a lighter touch, and to avoid overcrowding, one of these

knots could be left as line work rather than being converted into ribbons as has been done in Designs 168 and 172 (see pages 141 and 144).

Free ends of ribbons can be extended and closed off with zoomorphic motifs or with a simple node (see Design 164, page 139). Ribbons can also be looped, twisted and curled (see Fig 16.8).

Fig 16.7 An embellished motif of two fish, with knots substituted for their outlines.

*Use a small or large heart to embellish
the joining point of two ribbons*

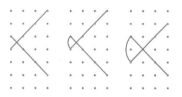

*Cross the ends of the ribbons to
form a small or large twist*

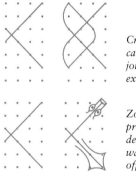

*Crossed ends
can also be
joined with an
extended loop*

*Zoomorphics
provide a
decorative
way to close
off a ribbon*

FIG 16.8 Alternative methods
of closing ribbons.

About the Author

Brought up during the war when few toys were available, Sheila was kept entertained with paper. Her father encouraged her to draw intricate patterns and make paper toys, and introduced her to the basic principles of paper engineering – a pastime which has become a lifetime pleasure.

She gives regular workshops in paper-related crafts for the County and Borough Councils, and in 1989 she was a runner-up in the BBC 2 Paper Engineering Competition.

Sheila is interested in many crafts. She enjoys designing and making automata, moving toys and tatting shuttles. Her collection of corn dollies and straw work is now on permanent display at Shuggborough Hall.

Her other interests include golf and playing the clarinet with a local concert band. She is a Parish Council Clerk, qualified music teacher and, together with a friend, runs a book-keeping service for local traders. Sheila lives in Lancashire with her husband and has three sons.

WOODCARVING

The Art of the Woodcarver   *GMC Publications*
Carving Architectural Detail in Wood: The Classical
Tradition   *Frederick Wilbur*
Carving Birds & Beasts   *GMC Publications*
Carving Nature: Wildlife Studies in Wood
    Frank Fox-Wilson
Carving Realistic Birds   *David Tippey*
Decorative Woodcarving   *Jeremy Williams*
Elements of Woodcarving   *Chris Pye*
Essential Tips for Woodcarvers   *GMC Publications*
Essential Woodcarving Techniques   *Dick Onians*
Further Useful Tips for Woodcarvers
    GMC Publications
Lettercarving in Wood: A Practical Course   *Chris Pye*
Making & Using Working Drawings for Realistic
Model Animals   *Basil F. Fordham*
Power Tools for Woodcarving   *David Tippey*

Practical Tips for Turners & Carvers
    GMC Publications
Relief Carving in Wood: A Practical Introduction
    Chris Pye
Understanding Woodcarving   *GMC Publications*
Understanding Woodcarving in the Round
    GMC Publications
Useful Techniques for Woodcarvers *GMC Publications*
Wildfowl Carving – Volume 1   *Jim Pearce*
Wildfowl Carving – Volume 2   *Jim Pearce*
Woodcarving: A Complete Course   *Ron Butterfield*
Woodcarving: A Foundation Course   *Zoë Gertner*
Woodcarving for Beginners   *GMC Publications*
Woodcarving Tools & Equipment Test Reports
    GMC Publications
Woodcarving Tools, Materials & Equipment *Chris Pye*

WOODTURNING

Adventures in Woodturning   *David Springett*
Bert Marsh: Woodturner   *Bert Marsh*
Bowl Turning Techniques Masterclass   *Tony Boase*
Colouring Techniques for Woodturners   *Jan Sanders*
Contemporary Turned Wood: New Perspectives in a
Rich Tradition *Ray Leier, Jan Peters & Kevin Wallace*
The Craftsman Woodturner   *Peter Child*
Decorative Techniques for Woodturners *Hilary Bowen*
Fun at the Lathe   *R.C. Bell*
Further Useful Tips for Woodturners
    GMC Publications
Illustrated Woodturning Techniques   *John Hunnex*
Intermediate Woodturning Projects *GMC Publications*
Keith Rowley's Woodturning Projects   *Keith Rowley*
Practical Tips for Turners & Carvers
    GMC Publications
Turning Green Wood   *Michael O'Donnell*
Turning Miniatures in Wood   *John Sainsbury*
Turning Pens and Pencils

    Kip Christensen & Rex Burningham
Understanding Woodturning   *Ann & Bob Phillips*
Useful Techniques for Woodturners *GMC Publications*
Useful Woodturning Projects   *GMC Publications*
Woodturning: Bowls, Platters, Hollow Forms, Vases,
Vessels, Bottles, Flasks, Tankards, Plates
    GMC Publications
Woodturning: A Foundation Course (New Edition)
    Keith Rowley
Woodturning: A Fresh Approach   *Robert Chapman*
Woodturning: An Individual Approach *Dave Regester*
Woodturning: A Source Book of Shapes *John Hunnex*
Woodturning Jewellery   *Hilary Bowen*
Woodturning Masterclass   *Tony Boase*
Woodturning Techniques   *GMC Publications*
Woodturning Tools & Equipment Test Reports
    GMC Publications
Woodturning Wizardry   *David Springett*

WOODWORKING

Adventures in Woodturning   *David Springett*
Bert Marsh: Woodturner   *Bert Marsh*
Bowl Turning Techniques Masterclass   *Tony Boase*
Colouring Techniques for Woodturners   *Jan Sanders*
Contemporary Turned Wood: New Perspectives in a
Rich Tradition *Ray Leier, Jan Peters & Kevin Wallace*
The Craftsman Woodturner   *Peter Child*
Decorative Techniques for Woodturners *Hilary Bowen*
Fun at the Lathe   *R.C. Bell*
Further Useful Tips for Woodturners
    GMC Publications
Illustrated Woodturning Techniques   *John Hunnex*
Intermediate Woodturning Projects *GMC Publications*
Keith Rowley's Woodturning Projects   *Keith Rowley*
Practical Tips for Turners & Carvers
    GMC Publications
Turning Green Wood   *Michael O'Donnell*
Turning Miniatures in Wood   *John Sainsbury*
Turning Pens and Pencils

    Kip Christensen & Rex Burningham
Understanding Woodturning   *Ann & Bob Phillips*
Useful Techniques for Woodturners *GMC Publications*
Useful Woodturning Projects   *GMC Publications*
Woodturning: Bowls, Platters, Hollow Forms, Vases,
Vessels, Bottles, Flasks, Tankards, Plates
    GMC Publications
Woodturning: A Foundation Course (New Edition)
    Keith Rowley
Woodturning: A Fresh Approach   *Robert Chapman*
Woodturning: An Individual Approach *Dave Regester*
Woodturning: A Source Book of Shapes *John Hunnex*
Woodturning Jewellery   *Hilary Bowen*
Woodturning Masterclass   *Tony Boase*
Woodturning Techniques   *GMC Publications*
Woodturning Tools & Equipment Test Reports
    GMC Publications
Woodturning Wizardry   *David Springett*

TOYMAKING

Designing & Making Wooden Toys — *Terry Kelly*
Fun to Make Wooden Toys & Games
Jeff & Jennie Loader
Restoring Rocking Horses
Clive Green & Anthony Dew

Scrollsaw Toy Projects — *Ivor Carlyle*
Scrollsaw Toys for All Ages — *Ivor Carlyle*
Wooden Toy Projects — *GMC Publications*

CRAFTS

American Patchwork Designs in Needlepoint
Melanie Tacon
A Beginners' Guide to Rubber Stamping *Brenda Hunt*
Blackwork: A New Approach *Brenda Day*
Celtic Cross Stitch Designs *Carol Phillipson*
Celtic Knotwork Designs *Sheila Sturrock*
Celtic Knotwork Handbook *Sheila Sturrock*
Celtic Spirals and Other Designs *Sheila Sturrock*
Collage from Seeds, Leaves and Flowers *Joan Carver*
Complete Pyrography *Stephen Poole*
Contemporary Smocking *Dorothea Hall*
Creating Colour with Dylon *Dylon International*
Creative Doughcraft *Patricia Hughes*
Creative Embroidery Techniques Using Colour
Through Gold *Daphne J. Ashby & Jackie Woolsey*
The Creative Quilter: Techniques and Projects
Pauline Brown
Decorative Beaded Purses *Enid Taylor*
Designing and Making Cards *Glennis Gilruth*
Glass Engraving Pattern Book *John Everett*
Glass Painting *Emma Sedman*
How to Arrange Flowers: A Japanese Approach to
English Design *Taeko Marvelly*
An Introduction to Crewel Embroidery *Mave Glenny*
Making and Using Working Drawings for Realistic
Model Animals *Basil F. Fordham*
Making Character Bears *Valerie Tyler*
Making Decorative Screens *Amanda Howes*

Making Fairies and Fantastical Creatures *Julie Sharp*
Making Greetings Cards for Beginners *Pat Sutherland*
Making Hand-Sewn Boxes: Techniques and Projects
Jackie Woolsey
Making Knitwear Fit *Pat Ashforth & Steve Plummer*
Making Mini Cards, Gift Tags & Invitations
Glennis Gilruth
Making Soft-Bodied Dough Characters
Patricia Hughes
Natural Ideas for Christmas: Fantastic Decorations to
Make *Josie Cameron-Ashcroft & Carol Cox*
Needlepoint: A Foundation Course *Sandra Hardy*
Patchwork for Beginners *Pauline Brown*
Pyrography Designs *Norma Gregory*
Pyrography Handbook (Practical Crafts)
Stephen Poole
Ribbons and Roses *Lee Lockheed*
Rose Windows for Quilters *Angela Besley*
Rubber Stamping with Other Crafts *Lynne Garner*
Sponge Painting *Ann Rooney*
Step-by-Step Pyrography Projects for the Solid Point
Machine *Norma Gregory*
Tassel Making for Beginners *Enid Taylor*
Tatting Collage *Lindsay Rogers*
Temari: A Traditional Japanese Embroidery Technique
Margaret Ludlow
Theatre Models in Paper and Card *Robert Burgess*
Wool Embroidery and Design *Lee Lockheed*

VIDEOS

Drop-in and Pinstuffed Seats *David James*
Stuffover Upholstery *David James*
Elliptical Turning *David Springett*
Woodturning Wizardry *David Springett*
Turning Between Centres: The Basics *Dennis White*
Turning Bowls *Dennis White*
Boxes, Goblets and Screw Threads *Dennis White*
Novelties and Projects *Dennis White*
Classic Profiles *Dennis White*

Twists and Advanced Turning *Dennis White*
Sharpening the Professional Way *Jim Kingshott*
Sharpening Turning & Carving Tools *Jim Kingshott*
Bowl Turning *John Jordan*
Hollow Turning *John Jordan*
Woodturning: A Foundation Course *Keith Rowley*
Carving a Figure: The Female Form *Ray Gonzalez*
The Router: A Beginner's Guide *Alan Goodsell*
The Scroll Saw: A Beginner's Guide *John Burke*

MAGAZINES

WOODTURNING ✦ WOODCARVING ✦ FURNITURE & CABINETMAKING
THE ROUTER ✦ WOODWORKING ✦ THE DOLLS' HOUSE MAGAZINE
WATER GARDENING ✦ EXOTIC GARDENING ✦ GARDEN CALENDAR
OUTDOOR PHOTOGRAPHY ✦ BUSINESSMATTERS

The above represents a selection of titles currently published or scheduled to be published.
All are available direct from the Publishers or through bookshops, newsagents and specialist retailers.
To place an order, or to obtain a complete catalogue, contact:

GMC PUBLICATIONS

Castle Place, 166 High Street, Lewes, East Sussex BN7 1XU, United Kingdom
Telephone: 01273 488005   Fax: 01273 478606   E-mail: pubs@thegmcgroup.com
Orders by credit card are accepted